More Joy to the World

Nancy Smith & Lynda Milligan

Book Production

Sharon Holmes – Editor, Technical Illustrator
Susan Johnson – Quilt & Project Designer, Photo Stylist
Lexie Foster – Graphic & Quilt Designer, Photography
Christine Scott – Editorial Assistant
Sandi Fruehling – Copy Reader
Brad Bartholomew – Photographer

Thanks

Sewers – Jane Dumler, Ann Petersen, Courtenay
Hughes, Katie Wells, Christine Scott, Kelly Kiel
Quilters – Ann Petersen, Jane Dumler, Merrie Martin Jones
Crate & Barrel – Photography in their beautiful store at
8505 Park Meadows Center Drive, Lone Tree, Colorado 80124

Every effort has been made to ensure that the information in this book is accurate. Due to individual skills, conditions, and tools, we cannot be responsible for any losses, injuries, or other damages that may result from its use.

POSSIBILITIES®

Fabric Designers for Avlyn, Inc. • Publishers of Possibilities® Books
Home of Great American Quilt Factory Inc.
www.greatamericanquilt.com • www.possibilitiesquilt.com
1.800.474.2665

Cookie Town

58 x 58″   Photo on page 3

Materials
Choose fabric with 40-42″ usable width.

Pinwheels	½ yd each of 2 dark blues
Tree backgrnd	⅝ yd light blue
Cookie backgrnd	⅝ yd light blue
Patchwork & applique	⅜ yd white
	⅓ yd each dark & med blue
	⅜ yd each dark & med green
	¼ yd each of 6 tans & browns
	¼ yd dark red
	⅛ yd each: 2 yellows
	⅙ yd each: 2 purples, 1 red
Sashing, Border 1	⅞ yd medium blue
Border 2	1 yd stripe - parallel to selvage
Border 2 corners	¼ yd
Binding	⅝ yd
Backing	3⅞ yd
Batting	64 x 64″
Trims	buttons, beads, ⅝″ white rickrack, embroidery floss, ¼″ ribbon

Cutting
Cut strips selvage to selvage.
*Cut in half diagonally.
Applique patterns on pages 41-43.

Pinwheels	*8 squares 6⅜″ of each fabric
Tree bkgrnd	5 pieces 8½ x 10″
Cookie bkg	5 pieces 9½ x 10″
House Block A	2 pieces 1½ x 12½″ - dk blue - side sky
	3 squares 3″ - dk blue - top sky
	2 squares 1¾″ - dk blue - top sky
	*1 square 3⅜″ - dk blue - sky by roof
	*1 square 3⅜″ - dark green - roof end
	*1 square 3⅜″ - medium green - roof side
	1 square 3″ - medium green - roof side
	2 squares 1¾″ - brown - chimneys
	1 piece 2½ x 5½″ - brown - door
	1 piece 2½ x 3½″ - yellow - window
	2 pieces 2 x 5½″ - brown - by door
	6 pieces 1½ x 5½″ - brown - under roof, under window
	2 pieces 2 x 3½″ - brown - by window
House Block B	2 pieces 1½ x 7½″ - med blue - side sky
	1 piece 1½ x 12½″ - med blue - top sky
	*1 square 4⅞″ - med blue - sky by roof
	*1 square 4⅞″ - dark purple - roof edge
	*1 square 4⅞″ - light purple - roof side
	2 squares 3½″ - brown - roof end
	1 piece 2½ x 5¾″ - brown - door
	1 square 4″ - yellow - window
	1 piece 2¼ x 10½″ - brown - under roof
	1 piece 2½ x 5¾″ - brown - by door
	2 pieces 1¾ x 4″ - brown - by window
	1 piece 6½ x 2¼″ - brown - under window

House Block C	2 pieces 2 x 6½″ - dk blue - side sky
	*1 square 6⅞″ - dk blue - top sky
	*1 square 6⅞″ - dark red - roof
	1 chimney - brown - pattern on page 41
	1 piece 2½ x 5½″ - brown - door
	2 squares 2½″ - yellow - windows
	2 pieces 2 x 5½″ - brown - by windows
	2 pieces 2½ x 3½″ - brown - under windows
	1 piece 1½ x 9½″ - brown - below roof
House Block D	1 piece 1½ x 7″ - med blue - top sky
	1 piece 1½ x 4″ - med blue - top sky
	2 squares 4″ - med blue - sky by roof
	1 piece 1½ x 2½″ - brown - chimney
	1 piece 4 x 12½″ - red - roof
	1 piece 2½ x 5¾″ - brown - door
	1 square 3½″ - yellow - window
	2 pieces 2¼ x 8″ - brown - by door
	1 piece 2½ x 2¾″ - brown - above door
	2 pieces 2¼ x 8″ - brown - by windows
	2 pieces 3½ x 2¾″ - brown - by windows
Sashing	2 pieces 1⅜ x 11½″ - Row 1
	3 pieces 1¼ x 11½″ - Row 1
	2 pieces 1½ x 10″ - Row 2
	4 pieces 2 x 10″ - Row 2
	4 pieces 1¼ x 10″ - Row 4
	4 strips 2½″ wide - horizontals
Border 1	5-6 strips 1½″ wide
Border 2	6 strips 4½″ wide
Border 2 corners	4 squares 4½″
Applique	4 snowflakes, 5 trees & stars, 2 wreaths, 13 candies, 5 cookies, 1 chimney, 1 large star, 2 hearts - trace directly from book
Binding	6-7 strips 2½″ wide

Directions
Use ¼″ seam allowance unless otherwise noted.

1. ROW 1: Make 4 blocks. Press. Applique snowflake to center of each. Stitch blocks and sashing pieces together with 2 wider sashing pieces on each end. Press.

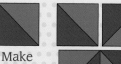

Make 16

Continued on page 11

Gingerbread Tree Skirt

52″ diameter   Photos on page 3 & back cover

Materials
Choose fabric with 40-42″ usable width.

Wedges	⅞ yd each of 3 fabrics
Ties	⅜ yd
Applique	⅛-⅓ yd pieces or scraps up to 9x16″
Binding	¾ yd
Backing	3⅜ yd
Batting	56x56″
Trims	1½″ white rickrack, buttons, beads, embroidery floss

Cutting
Cut strips selvage to selvage.
Wedge pattern on page 46.
Applique patterns on pages 41-42.

Wedges   6 from each fabric - fold fabric in half parallel to selvage & cut 3 wedges

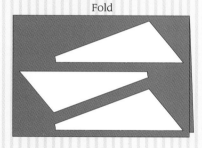

Fold

Ties   4 pieces 4½x20″

Applique   1 house, 2 trees, 4 gingerbread men, 3 candies, 2 hearts - trace directly from book

Binding   **bias** strips 2½″ wide pieced to 250″ long

Directions
Use ¼″ seam allowance unless otherwise noted.

1. WEDGES: Pair wedges as shown and make 9 units. Press. Stitch into complete tree skirt, leaving 1 seam open. Press.

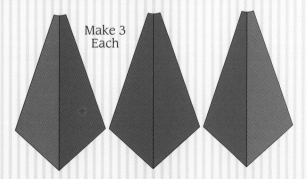

Make 3 Each

2. APPLIQUE: Stitch appliques in positions shown, keeping them an inch or more from raw edges. Stitch rickrack to lower edge of roof.

Leave Open

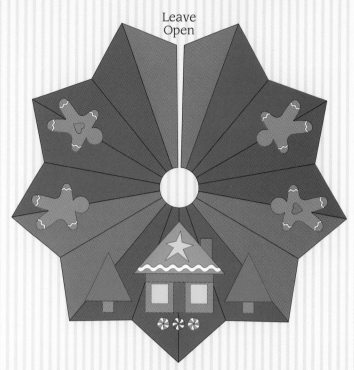

3. LAYER & QUILT: Piece backing to same size as batting. Layer and quilt as desired. Trim backing and batting to same size and shape as top, including back and center openings.

4. TIES: Fold each tie in half lengthwise, right sides together. Stitch long edge and one short edge. Turn right side out. Press. Pleat unfinished end to make it narrower. Baste unfinished ends in positions shown, raw edges even. Note that ties nearest center are an inch or so from raw edge of center hole.

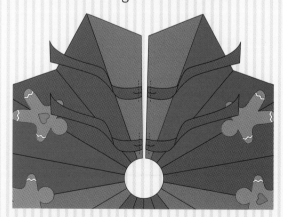

5. BIND & ADD TRIMS: Stitch binding strips end to end. Press in half lengthwise, wrong sides together. Bind tree skirt using ⅜″ seam allowance, pivoting at each inside point and mitering each outside point. Stitch buttons and/or beads to gingerbread men, trees, and house. Embroider mouths on gingerbread men.

Hearthstone

64 x 64"   10½" Block   Photo on page 7

Yardage
Choose fabric with 40-42" usable width.

Blocks, sashing,
Border 2
- ¼ yd each of 3 dark reds
- ½ yd each of 3 medium reds
- ⅙ yd each of 3 dark tans
- ⅙ yd each of 3 tans
- ⅓ yd peachy tan
- ⅝ yd tan check
- ⅜ yd green
- ⅙ yd cream
- ⅜ yd cream/tan print

Strip sets for
sashing, Bdr 2   ¼ yd each - 1 dark red, 2 dark tans, 2 light tans

Setting triangles   1 yd
Borders 1 & 3   ½ yd
Border 4   ⅞ yd
Binding   ⅝ yd
Backing   4¼ yd
Batting   70 x 70"

Cutting
Cut strips selvage to selvage.
*Cut in half diagonally.
**Cut in quarters diagonally.

Blocks, sashing, Border 2
dark reds	36 squares 2"
	*36 squares 2⅜"
medium reds	90 squares 2"
	*108 squares 2⅜"
dark tans	*36 squares 2⅜"
tans	*36 squares 2⅜"
peachy tan	36 pieces 2 x 3½"
tan check	6 strips 2" wide - strip sets
	40 squares 2"
green	53 squares 2"
cream	16 pieces 2 x 3½"
cream/tan	16 squares 5"
Strip sets	3 strips 2" wide of each fabric
Setting triangles	*2 squares 10½"
	**2 squares 18¼"
Borders 1 & 3	12 strips 1" wide
Border 4	7 strips 3½" wide
Binding	7 strips 2½" wide

Directions
Use ¼" seam allowance unless otherwise noted.

1. BLOCKS: Make 13 blocks as shown. In red block, tan/medium red units go closest to tan check square. Dark tan/medium red units go on corners. Press.

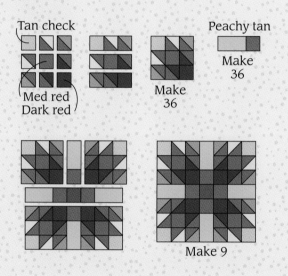

Make 72 - tans & med reds

Make 72 - dark tans & med reds

Make 72 - dark reds & med reds

Tan check   Peachy tan

Med red
Dark red   Make 36   Make 36

Make 9

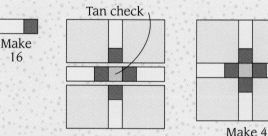

Make 16   Tan check   Make 4

2. SASHING/BORDER 3 STRIP SETS: Make 3 strip sets as shown. Use 2 different dark tan and 2 different tan strips in each set. Place tan check in all strip sets as shown. Press. Crosscut into 2" segments.

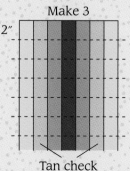

Make 3

2"

Tan check

Continued on page 13

Gingerbread Wall Quilt   p 8
Hot Pads   p 9

Holly Wreath   p 23
Felted Ornaments   p 12

Gingerbread Wall Quilt

23x46"   10" Block   Photo on page 7

Materials
Choose fabric with 40-42" usable width.

Applique	backgrnd	⅜ yd each of 2 tans
	cookies	¼ yd each of 2 tans
	others	⅛ yd pieces or scraps up to 3x3"
Sashing		⅙ yd each of red, tan, brown
Borders 1 & 3		⅓ yd green
Border 2		¼ yd dark brown
Border 3		⅜ yd red stripe - parallel to selvage
Binding		⅜ yd
Backing		1½ yd
Batting		27x50"
Trims		buttons, beads & embroidery floss

Cutting
Cut strips selvage to selvage.
*Cut in half diagonally.
Applique patterns on pages 40, 41.

Applique	backgrnd	3 squares 10½"
	others	3 gingerbread men, 1 heart, 4 stars - trace directly from book
Sashing	red	8 squares 2"
		*16 squares 2⅜"
	brown	*16 squares 2⅜"
	tan	8 pieces 2x4½"
		2 pieces 2x10½"
Border 1		3 strips 2" wide - green
Border 2		3 strips 1¼" wide
Border 3		3 strips 3½" wide
	corners	4 squares 3½" - green
Binding		4 strips 2½" wide

Directions
Use ¼" seam allowance unless otherwise noted.

1. BLOCKS: Applique 3 blocks, keeping pieces out of seam allowance. Applique 4 corner squares.

Make 1   Make 2    Make 4

2. SASHING: Make 32 half-square triangle units. Press. Use triangle units and 2x4½" tan rectangles to make vertical and horizontal sashing pieces. Press.

 Make 32

Make 4 - Verticals

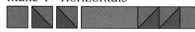

Make 4 - Horizontals

3. ASSEMBLE: Stitch vertical sashing to sides of top and bottom blocks, 2x10½" tan rectangles to sides of center block. Press. Stitch blocks and horizontal sashing together. Press.

4. BORDERS 1 & 2: Cut 2 strips to same length as quilt. Stitch to sides of quilt. Press. Repeat at top and bottom.

5. BORDER 3: Cut 2 strips to same length as quilt. Cut 2 strips to same width as quilt. Stitch corner squares to each end of short border pieces. Press. Stitch long borders to sides of quilt. Stitch short borders to top and bottom of quilt. Press.

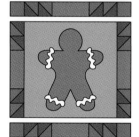

6. LAYER & QUILT: Cut backing to same size as batting. Layer and quilt as desired. Trim backing and batting even with top.

7. BIND & ADD TRIMS: Stitch binding strips end to end. Press in half lengthwise, wrong sides together. Bind quilt using ⅜" seam allowance. Stitch buttons, beads, and mouths to gingerbread men.

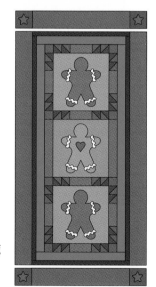

Gingerbread Apron

Photo on page 5

Materials
Choose fabric with 40-42″ usable width.

Apron, lining	1¾ yd blue
Pocket	⅓ yd red
Ties, pocket	⅜ yd red stripe - parallel to selvage
Appliques	⅛-⅙ yd pieces or scraps up to 5x8″
Trims	¼″ & ⅝″ white rickrack, buttons, beads, embroidery floss

Cutting
Cut strips selvage to selvage.
Applique patterns on inside back cover.

Blue	cut 2 using apron pattern, page 47	
Red	pocket	1 piece 6½x16½″ - outside
		1 piece 8½x16½″ - lining
Stripe	pocket	1 piece 2½x16½″
	ties	3 strips 2½″
Applique	1 house, 1 star, 2 trees, 2 gingerbread men, 3 candies - trace directly from book	

Directions
Use ¼″ seam allowance unless otherwise noted.

1. POCKET: Stitch red piece for outside and stripe piece together on long sides. Press. For pockets, mark 3 vertical lines lightly with pencil, 1 in center and 1 to each side of center, 4″ away. Applique gingerbread men and trees on marked panels, keeping appliques out of ¼″ seam allowance at each side. Stitch ¼″ rickrack to arms and legs. Stitch beads to chest, and add face. Place pocket and pocket lining right sides together. Stitch around pocket, leaving opening on bottom edge for turning. Trim corners, turn right side out, and press.

2. APRON: Applique house 2″ down from top edge, centered from side to side. Stitch ⅝″ rickrack to roof and buttons to windows of house. Pin pocket to apron 5¼″ from bottom edge, centered from side to side. Topstitch side and bottom edges. Stitch on pencil lines, creating 4 pockets. Applique candies at top of each pocket stitching line.

3. FINISH: Follow Steps 3-4 on page 32 for finishing apron.

Tea Towels & Hot Pads

Photos on pages 5, 7, 27

Use our applique patterns to make coordinating sets of tea towels and hot pads. These items make thoughtful gifts for friends and relatives during the holidays.

Start with purchased towels and hot pads.

TEA TOWELS
Cut 4-4½″ strips for each end of towel. Vary width of strips with thickness of towel. Press ¼″ to wrong side on each long end of strip. Press strip in half, wrong sides together. Unfold and position end of towel near fold. Fold ends of strip in and press in place. Refold strip over towel and pin securely. Stitch folded edge with zigzag or machine blanket stitch. Hand stitch ends. Add appliques in fabrics that coordinate with towels.

HOT PADS
Add appliques in fabrics that coordinate with hot pads.

Casserole Carrier

For 9x13″ baking dish   Photos on pages 5, 27

Materials   Choose fabric with 42″ usable width.

Panels	end panel	⅜ yd
	end panel lining	⅜ yd
	side panel	½ yd
	side panel lining	½ yd
Appliques		⅛-¼ yd pieces or scraps up to 7x7″
Batting, thin cotton		28x45″
Trims	gingerbread man	beads, ¼″ white rickrack, embroidery floss
	poinsettia	beads
Dowels		2 - 18″ long, ⅝″ diameter - paint if desired
Velcro® strip		¼ yd

Cutting   Gingerbread man pattern on inside back cover
Poinsettia pattern on page 45

Panels	1 piece 10½x41½″ - end panel
	1 piece 10½x41½″ - end panel lining
	1 piece 14½x32½″ - side panel
	1 piece 14½x32½″ - side panel lining
Appliques	2 gingerbread men, 2 background squares 5″ OR
	2 poinsettias, 6 leaves - trace directly from book
Batting	1 piece 10½x41½″ - end panel
	1 piece 14½x32½″ - side panel

Directions
Use ¼″ seam allowance unless otherwise noted.

1. END PANEL: Place end panel pieces right sides together on top of end panel batting. Stitch around all four sides, leaving an opening on one long side for turning. Clip corners, turn right side out, and press. Whipstitch opening closed. Machine quilt lines parallel to long edges.

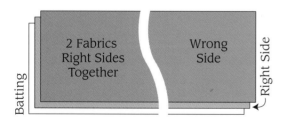

2. SIDE PANEL: Applique gingerbread men and background squares—or poinsettias—on each short end of side panel fabric 4½″ down and centered from side to side.

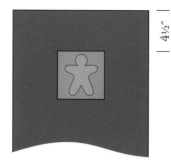

Make template of handle opening guide, page 45. Fold side panel lining piece in half lengthwise, right sides together (7¼x32½″). Place template along center fold. Mark handle opening on wrong side of each end of side lining piece. Repeat on other side of fold on each end to complete the U shape.

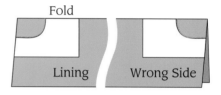

Place side panel pieces right sides together, then place on top of side panel batting, lining piece with handle markings facing up.

Stitch around all four sides and along marked lines for handle openings, leaving an opening on one side for turning. Cut out handle openings, leaving ¼″ seam allowance. Clip, turn, and press as in Step 1. Mark and quilt as before, stopping quilting lines when they meet appliques. Quilt close to appliques.

Fold 2″ of each end to inside to form casings. Topstitch in place. Repeat on other side.

Continued on page 12

Cookie Town

Continued from page 2

2. ROW 2: Applique trees to background pieces, bottom edge of trunk even with raw edge of background. Stitch blocks and sashing pieces together with 2 narrower sashing pieces on each end. Stitch horizontal sashing strips end to end. Press. Cut 3 pieces 48½" long. Stitch one to top and one to bottom of tree row. Press. Applique stars to tops of trees.

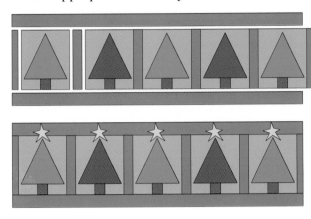

3. ROW 3: Make 4 house blocks, adding rickrack, chimney, wreaths, and star as shown. Press.

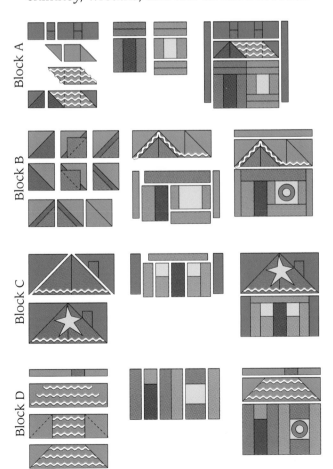

Stitch blocks into a row. Press. Stitch remaining horizontal sashing strip to bottom. Press. Applique candies. Directions on page 41.

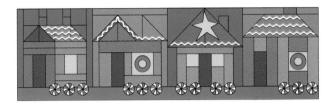

4. ROW 4: Applique cookies to background pieces, keeping them out of seam allowances. Stitch blocks and sashing pieces together. Press.

Make 3   Make 2

5. ASSEMBLE: Stitch rows together. Press.

6. BORDER 1: Stitch strips end to end. Press. Cut 2 pieces the same length as quilt. Stitch to sides of quilt. Press. Repeat at top and bottom.

Continued on page 12

Cookie Town

Continued from page 11

7. BORDER 2: Stitch strips end to end. Press. Cut 4 pieces the same length/width as quilt. Stitch one to each side of quilt. Press. Stitch corner squares to each end of remaining pieces. Press. Stitch to top and bottom of quilt. Press.

8. LAYER & QUILT: Piece backing to same size as batting. Layer and quilt as desired. Trim backing and batting even with top.

9. BIND & ADD TRIMS: Stitch binding strips end to end. Press in half lengthwise, wrong sides together. Bind quilt using ⅜" seam allowance. Tack ribbon bows to wreaths. Stitch beads, buttons, and mouths to cookies. Stitch buttons to trees and windows.

Casserole Carrier

Continued from page 10

3. FINISH: With lining sides up, place end panel on top of side panel at right angles, centered in both directions. Stitch around rectangle formed by crossover. Double stitch for strength.

Stitch beads and rickrack to gingerbread men. Embroider faces. Stitch beads to centers of poinsettias.

Cut 2 pieces of Velcro® 4½" long. Stitch to corners of end panel as shown.

Insert dowels into casings for handles.

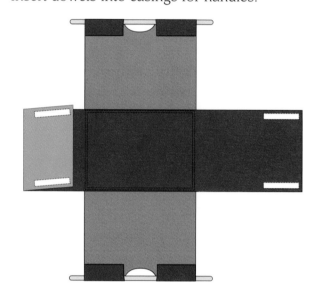

Felted Ornaments

Photos on pages 3, 5, 7, 19, 29

Materials for Each Gingerbread Man Ornament: 4¼ x 5" piece of brown, tan, or white wool felt; brown wool roving; ¼" white rickrack; beads for eyes and buttons; ¼" ribbon for neck bow and hanger.

Required Tools: Felting needle tool and felting needle mat. See directions with tools for learning the technique.

Cut gingerbread man out of felt. Pattern on inside back cover.

Felt both sides of gingerbread man. The first side felted will be the front and have a fuzzy, soft texture made by the ends of the fibers punched through when the back side is felted.

Machine stitch rickrack to arms and legs. Stitch beads to ornament. Hand stitch a loop of ribbon to top.

Hearthstone

Continued from page 6

3. SASHING: Stitch sashing units and green squares to blocks as shown. Press.

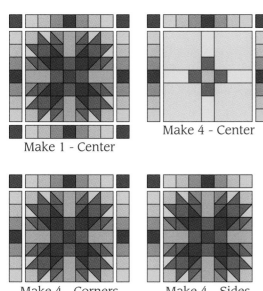

Make 1 - Center

Make 4 - Center

Make 4 - Corners

Make 4 - Sides

4. ASSEMBLE: Place blocks and side setting triangles in position.

Stitch blocks and setting triangles into diagonal rows. Press. Stitch rows together. Press. Stitch corner triangles to quilt. Press.

5. BORDER 1: Stitch strips end to end. Press. Cut 2 to same length as quilt. Stitch to sides of quilt. Press. Repeat at top and bottom.

6. BORDER 2: Use remaining strip set segments to make borders as shown at bottom of page. Press. Stitch side borders to quilt. Press. Stitch top and bottom borders to quilt. Press. Note: Photo varies slightly from directions. Refer to diagrams for making these borders and stitching them to quilt.

7. BORDERS 3 & 4: Repeat Step 5.

8. LAYER & QUILT: Piece backing to same size as batting. Layer and quilt as desired. Trim backing and batting even with top.

9. BIND: Stitch binding strips end to end. Press in half lengthwise, wrong sides together. Bind quilt using ⅜″ seam allowance.

Sides - Make 2 - 5 segments + 5 green squares

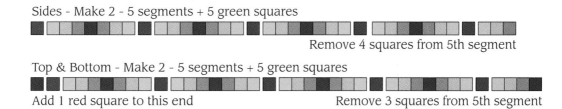

Remove 4 squares from 5th segment

Top & Bottom - Make 2 - 5 segments + 5 green squares

Add 1 red square to this end   Remove 3 squares from 5th segment

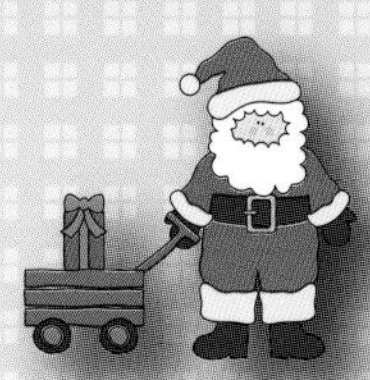

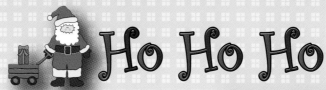

Ho Ho Ho

40x40″ Photo on page 15

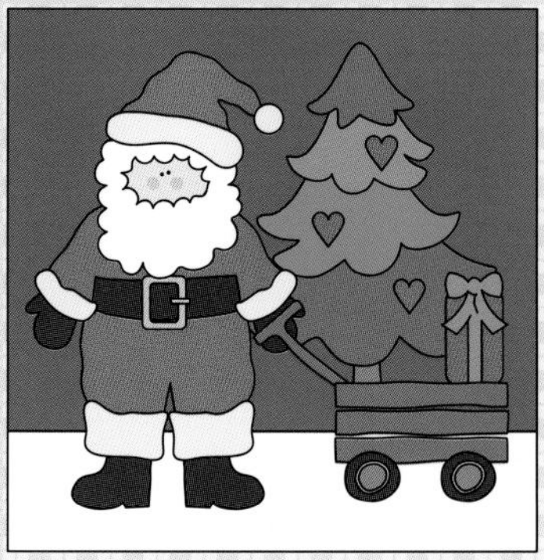

Materials

Choose fabric with 40-42″ usable width.

Applique	sky	½ yd blue
	snow	¼ yd white
	others	⅛-⅓ yd pieces or scraps up to 9x9″
Border 1		¼ yd red
Borders 2 & 4		⅙ yd each of 15 or more reds - mediums & darks
		⅞ yd white
		⅙ yd red - Border 2 corner blocks
		¼ yd red - Border 4 corner squares
Border 3		¼ yd green
Binding		½ yd
Backing		2¾ yd
Batting		44x44″
Trims		embroidery floss

Cutting

Cut strips selvage to selvage.
Applique patterns on pages 40, 44.
Border 2 paper piecing patterns on pages 39, 47.

Backgrnd	1 piece 18½x14½″ - blue
	1 piece 18½x4½″ - white
Applique	make **200% copies** of Santa, tree, wagon, & gift, then trace - trace star, hearts for tree & corner squares directly from book
Border 1	3 strips 1½″ wide
Borders 2, 4	Corner blocks Border 2:
	2 strips 1½″ wide each of white & red
	Paper-piecing side units Border 2:
	44 pieces 3x6″ - white
	Reds for Borders 2 & 4:
	40 pieces 3x6″ - paper piecing Bdr 2
	1½″ wide strips - Border 4
	cut 2-3 pieces across end of each 6″-wide piece for Bdr 2, leaving a piece approximately 32x6″ for cutting 2-3 strips 1½″ wide for Bdr 4 (leave more of the darks for Border 4)

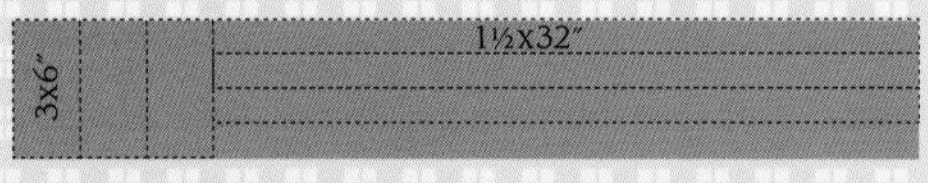
3x6″
1½x32″

Border 3	4 strips 1½″ wide
Border 4	4 squares 5½″ - corner squares
Binding	5 strips 2½″ wide

Directions

Use ¼″ seam allowance unless otherwise noted.

1. BACKGROUND & APPLIQUE: Stitch sky and snow together to make 18½″ square. Press. Position all appliques except star using photo and diagrams as guides. Fuse and stitch. Embroider eyes.
2. BORDER 1: Cut 2 pieces 18½″ long and stitch one to each side of center panel. Press. Repeat at top and bottom with pieces cut 20½″ long.
3. BORDER 2:
Corner Blocks: Make 1 strip set with red and white 1½″ strips, as shown. Press. Crosscut into 16 segments 1½″ wide. Stitch segments, rotated as shown, into 4 blocks. Press.

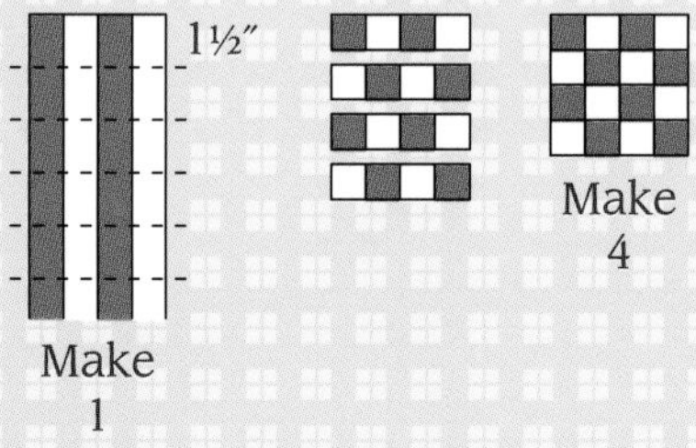
1½″
Make 1
Make 4

Side Borders: Paper piece 4 left end sections, 4 right end sections, and 8 center sections. Assemble as shown into 4 borders. Stitch one to each side of quilt oriented as shown. Press. Stitch corner blocks to each end of remaining borders. Press. Stitch to top and bottom of quilt. Press. Another diagram on page 24.

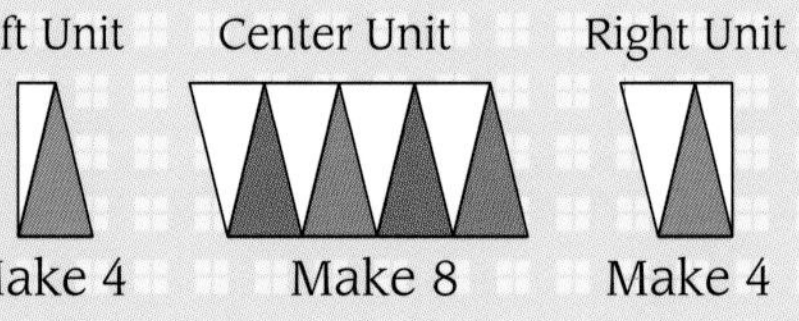
Left Unit
Center Unit
Right Unit
Make 4
Make 8
Make 4

Sides - Make 2

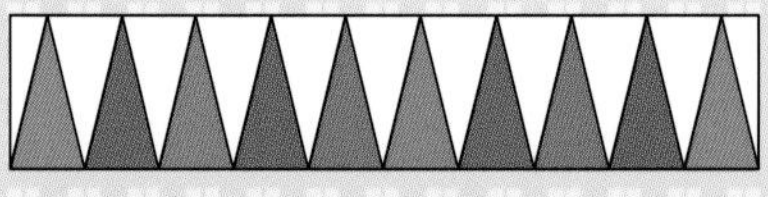

Top & Bottom - Make 2

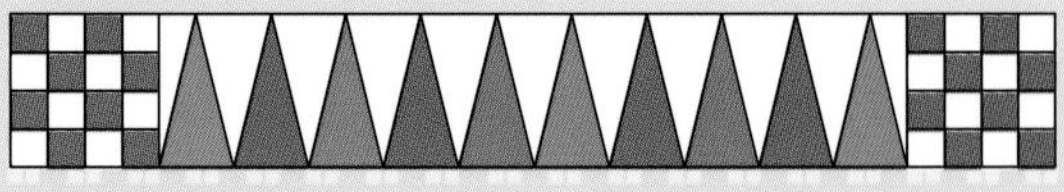

Continued on page 24

Ho Ho Ho   p 14
Stockings   p 22

15

Snowberries

60x75″ 12″ Block Photo on page 17

Yardage
Choose fabric with 40-42″ usable width.

Blocks, sashing,
  Border 2   ¼ yd each of 24 reds
Blocks, sashing,
  Borders 1 & 2   3 yd white
Border 3   ⅞ yd red
Binding   ⅔ yd
Backing   4¾ yd
Batting   66x81″

Cutting
Cut strips selvage to selvage.
  *Cut in half diagonally.
  Patterns on page 38.

Reds   24 Piece A - 1 of each fabric - blocks
         24 Piece D - 1 of each fabric - blocks
         96 squares 3½″ - 4 of each fabric - blocks -
           paper piecing of Piece B
         *144 squares 2⅞″ - 6 of each fabric - blocks
         31 pieces 2x12½″ - 1-2 of each fabric - sashing
         *78 squares 2⅜″ - 3-4 of each fabric - Border 2
         4 squares 2″ - Border 2 corners
White   3 strips 5″ wide - Border 1 sides
         3 strips 5¾″ wide - Border 1 top/bottom
         24 Piece C - blocks, pattern on page 38
         72 pieces 2½x3½″ - blocks - paper piecing of
           Piece B
         *72 squares 2⅞″ - blocks
         20 squares 2″ - sashing
         *78 squares 2⅜″ - Border 2
Border 3 7 strips 3½″ wide
Binding   7-8 strips 2½″ wide

Directions
Use ¼″ seam allowance unless otherwise noted.

1. BLOCKS
   Corner Units: Make 144 half-square triangle
   units. Press. Using 3 half-square units and 3
   additional red triangles, make 48 corner units.
   Press.

     Make 144

   Corner Units
   Make 48

Center Units: Paper piece 24 Piece B. Press.
Stitch pieces A-D together. Press. Stitch 2
corner units to each center unit. Press.

Center
Units
Make
24

Half Blocks
Make 24

Finish Blocks: Stitch half-blocks together into
blocks. Press.

Make 12

2. ASSEMBLE: Stitch white sashing squares and
   red sashing rectangles into rows. Press. Stitch
   sashing rectangles and blocks into rows. Press.
   Stitch rows together. Press.

16

Continued on page 25

Snowberries   p 16

Door Topper

11 x 32″ Photos on pages 5, 19

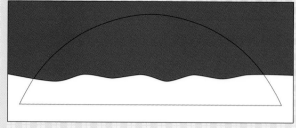

Materials
Choose fabric with 40-42″ usable width.

Fabric	background	½ yd
	snow	¼ yd
	appliques	⅛ yd pieces or scraps
	backing, pocket	⅞ yd
	binding	⅓ yd
Batting		14 x 34″
Poster board		1 piece
Trims	Santa	embroidery floss, blush makeup
	Gingerbread	beads, embroidery floss, ¼″ & ⅝″ white rickrack

Cutting
Applique patterns on pages 40, 44 & inside back cover. Trace directly from book.

Background	1 piece 14 x 34″
Snow	1 piece 5½ x 34″
Appliques	choose from diagrams below
Backing, pocket	2 pieces 14 x 34″
Binding	**bias** strips 2½″ wide to make 80″ long when stitched end to end
Poster board	1 piece using line on pattern

Directions
Use ¼″ seam allowance unless otherwise noted.

1. PATTERN: Make full-sized pattern (page 48). Cut out pattern on outside line.

2. MARK BACKGROUND & APPLIQUE: Back snow rectangle and other appliques with fusible web. Cut a gentle curve on top edge of snow. Fuse snow to background piece with bottom edges even. Place pattern on right side of background/snow rectangle, centered in both directions, and draw a line around it. Arrange appliques (also rickrack on roof and gingerbread men). Fuse and stitch.

3. LAYER & QUILT: Layer appliqued piece with batting and one of the backing rectangles. Quilt as desired. Cut out Topper on line drawn in Step 2. Embroider faces. Stitch beads to gingerbread men. Use blush makeup on Santa's cheeks.

4. POCKET: Cut a pocket using quilted piece as a pattern. Hem bottom edge of pocket with a ¾″ single-fold hem. Baste hemmed pocket piece and quilted piece, wrong sides together, along curved edge, leaving hemmed edge free.

5. BINDING: Stitch binding strips together end to end. Press in half lengthwise, wrong sides together. Bind Topper with a ⅜″ seam allowance, mitering bottom corners.

6. POSTER BOARD: Slide poster board into pocket. Hand stitch bottom edge of pocket to backing of quilted piece or tack at intervals.

Santa Door Topper

Gingerbread Door Topper

Punchneedle Ornaments

Photos on pages 19, 29

Materials for Each Ornament: Square of weaver's cloth big enough for hoop, 4½" square of black felt, embroidery floss in desired colors, ribbon for hanger. **Required Tools:** Punchneedle and no-slip embroidery hoop. See directions with punchneedle tool for learning the technique.

Trace quilt block ornament to weaver's cloth. For tree, wagon, or Santa ornament, trace checkerboard frame, then trace desired shape in center on diagonal, overlapping checkerboard when necessary. Use 2 strands of floss. When punching is finished, trim weaver's cloth, leaving ½" all around ornament. Make Santa's eyes with French knots. Turn ½" to back and hand stitch to felt. Use pinking shears to trim edge of felt. Hand stitch ribbon hanger to top.

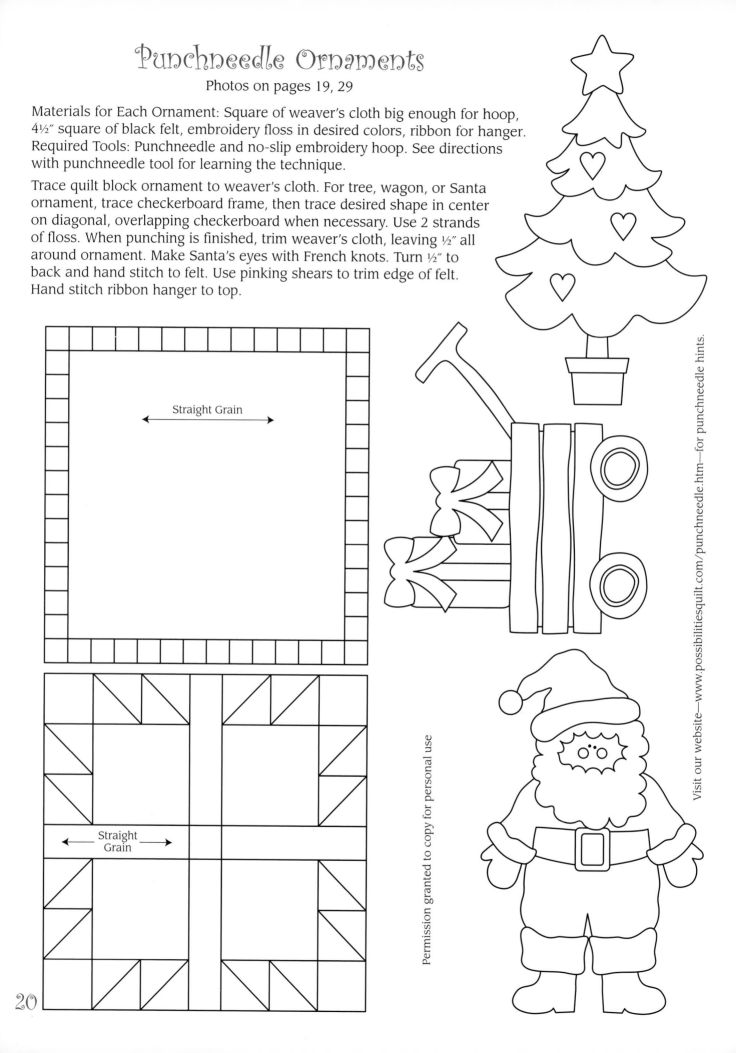

Straight Grain

Straight Grain

Visit our website—www.possibilitiesquilt.com/punchneedle.htm—for punchneedle hints.

Santa Card Hanger

14x47″   Photo on page 19

Materials
Choose fabric with 40-42″ usable width.

Blues	dark	½ yd - pocket background, Santa background
	med 1&2	¼ yd each of 2 - pockets
	med 3	⅜ yd - top triangle, Santa background
Green	light	⅙ yd - sashing
	med	⅜ yd - prairie points
Red	dark	⅙ yd - border
Appliques		⅛-¼ yd pieces or scraps up to 8x8″
Backing, facing		1⅜ yd
Batting		18x51″
Hanger		½″ ribbon
Trims		embroidery floss, blush makeup

Cutting
Cut strips selvage to selvage.
*Cut in half diagonally.
Applique patterns on pages 40, 42-44.

Blues	dark	4 pieces 6½x12½″ - pocket bkg
		1 piece 9½x8″ - Santa backgrnd
	med 1&2	4 squares 6½″ of each fabric
	med 3	*1 square 10⅞″ - top triangle
		2 pieces 2x8″ - Santa backgrnd
		1 piece 2x12½″ - Santa backgrnd
Green	light	4 pieces 1¾x12½″ - sashing
	med	32 squares 3″ - prairie points
Red	dark	3 strips 1½″ wide
Facing		3 strips 1½″ wide
Appliques		Santa, wagon, gift, tree, tree star, 4 spiky stars, snowflake - trace all directly from book

Directions
Use ¼″ seam allowance unless otherwise noted.

1. POCKET UNITS: Stitch two 6½″ squares, one of each fabric, together on 2 adjacent sides. Trim point. Press seam allowances open as close to point as possible. Fold so seam is at center. Press. Applique star to center. Baste pocket to background at bottom edge. Tip of pocket should be ¼″ from raw edge of background. Stitch pocket to background along vertical seam, skipping over the star, and backstitching at top point.

2. ASSEMBLE: Stitch pocket units, sashing and Santa background together as shown. Press. Cut border strips to same length as hanger. Stitch to sides of hanger. Press. Repeat at top and bottom. Stitch top triangle to hanger. Press.

3. APPLIQUE: Applique Santa, wagon, gift, and tree at bottom of hanger. Applique snowflake to top triangle, overlapping seam with red border and keeping it out of seam allowance along top edges.

4. LAYER & QUILT: Piece backing to same size as batting. Layer and quilt as desired. Trim backing and batting even with top.

5. PRAIRIE POINTS: Fold and press 32 prairie points for edging. Diagrams on page 23. Pin prairie points to long sides of card hanger, raw edges even, slipping one inside the next to space them evenly. They will overlap each other close to the ¼″ seam line. At each end, folded edge of prairie point should match seam intersection so corner will be smooth when turned. Baste prairie points in place ³⁄₁₆″ from edge. Diagrams on page 23.

6. FACING: Stitch facing strips end to end. Press seam allowances open. Press ½″ to wrong side on one long edge. Place unpressed edge of facing strip right sides together with raw edge of hanger and pivoting at

Continued on page 23

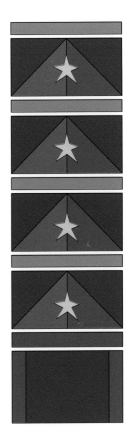

Stockings

20″ Photos on pages 5, 15, 29

Materials
Choose fabric with 40-42″ usable width.

Stocking	⅔ yd
Cuff	¼ yd sherpa
Lining	⅔ yd
Appliques	⅛-⅓ yd pieces or scraps up to 12x12″
Thin batting	2 pieces 15x24″
	cotton blend or bonded polyester
Hanger	¼ yd ⅝″-wide ribbon, ⅝-¾″ button
Trims	buttons, beads, embroidery floss
	cookie girl - ⅝″ ribbon for head bow

Cutting
Stocking pattern on page 48. Make **200% copies**. Applique patterns on pages 40-45, 47.

Stocking	2 pieces 15x24″
Cuff	2 pieces from pattern
Lining	1 & 1 reversed from pattern
Appliques	make **200% copies** of gingerbread man, tree, or Santa, then trace - trace poinsettia directly from book

Directions
Use ⅜″ seam allowance unless otherwise noted.

1. FRONT: Mark around stocking pattern on right side of one stocking rectangle. Fuse appliques using photos and diagrams as guides for placement. Place fused stocking rectangle wrong side down on batting. Applique. Mark cutting line for stocking over appliques. Cut stocking out on line. Add trims, keeping them out of seam allowance.

2. BACK: Layer remaining stocking rectangle and batting, as before. Quilt. **Reverse pattern** for stocking back. Mark cutting line and cut out.

3. ASSEMBLE: With right sides together, stitch curved edges of stocking front and back. Trim seam allowance and clip curves. Turn stocking right side out. Repeat with lining pieces using ⅝″ seam allowance. Place lining in stocking, wrong sides together, and baste along top edge.

4. CUFF: Applique name on front cuff, if desired. Place approximately 1″ above bottom edge. Use tip of iron only (or a mini iron) on letter fabric to avoid flattening sherpa. Reduce or enlarge letters on a photocopier for desired size, and/or overlap edges of letters to make name fit. The short names on the stockings in the photos were done at 200%. Stitch side seams of front and back cuff pieces. Place cuff inside top of stocking, lining side of stocking to right side of cuff. Match and pin top raw edges. Stitch. Turn cuff to outside of stocking. Fluff sherpa over cut edge at bottom of cuff.

5. HANGER: Cut an 8″ piece of ribbon and trim ends on diagonal. Make a loop and stitch to top of stocking by sewing through button placed on top.

22

Holly Wreath

18″ Photos on pages 3, 7, 19

Photos on pages 3 and 7 have 5 felted ornaments.
See page 12 for felted ornament directions.

Materials
Choose fabric with 40-42″ usable width.

Leaf fabrics	⅞ yd each of 4
Wrapping fabric	⅝ yd
Bow fabric	¼ yd
Fusible web	5 yd
Straw wreath	14″ diameter
Red berries	5-7 clusters - optional
Template plastic	
Tacky fabric glue	

Cutting

Leaf fabrics	4 strips 7″ wide from each
Wrapping fabric	4 strips 4″ wide
Bow fabric	1 strip 6½″ wide
Fusible web	8 pieces a bit smaller than fabric strips

Directions
Use ¼″ seam allowance unless otherwise noted.

1. MAKE TEMPLATE: Make plastic template from pattern on this page.

2. MAKE DOUBLE-SIDED FABRIC: Divide leaf fabric strips into pairs, mixing up the colors. Following manufacturer's directions, fuse web to wrong sides of 8 strips of fabric. Peel off paper and fuse remaining 8 strips of fabric, wrong side down, on web side of first 8 strips.

3. TRACE & CUT OUT LEAVES: Trace around holly leaf template on double-sided fabric strips. Cut out.

4. PUSH LEAVES INTO WREATH: Wrap 4″ strips around wreath and glue ends in place. Cut a slit in fabric wrap with a craft knife. Wrap center of leaf unit around point of dull knife or letter opener. Dab glue on point and push leaf into straw wreath through slit in fabric wrap. Place an equal number of leaves in each quadrant of wreath.

5. BOW: Fold strip in half lengthwise, right sides together. Cut each end on the diagonal. Stitch raw edges, leaving an opening at center for turning. Clip corners and turn right side out. Press. Tie a bow and attach to wreath.

6. FINISH: Attach berry clusters or felted ornaments to wreath.

Permission granted to copy for personal use.

Santa Card Hanger

Continued from page 21

seam intersections of corners. Trim corners. Fold facing to back of hanger so prairie points extend at edge. Hand stitch pressed edge to back of hanger, mitering corners.

7. ADD TRIMS & HANGING LOOP: Add eyes with floss and cheeks with makeup. Tack a loop of ribbon to back of card hanger at point of top triangle.

Place Christmas cards in pockets!

Ho Ho Ho

Continued from page 14

Finish Applique: Stitch star to top of tree, over-lapping seam.

4. BORDER 3: Cut 2 pieces 28½" long and stitch one to each side of quilt. Press. Repeat at top and bottom with pieces cut 30½" long.

5. BORDER 4:
Crosscut strips:

Centers		24 squares 1½"
1	Round 1 lights	24 squares 1½"
2	Round 1 darks	24 pieces 1½ x 2½"
3		24 pieces 1½ x 2½"
4	Round 1 lights	24 pieces 1½ x 3½"
5	Round 2 lights	24 pieces 1½ x 3½"
6	Round 2 darks	24 pieces 1½ x 4½"
7		24 pieces 1½ x 4½"
8	Round 2 lights	24 pieces 1½ x 5½"

Using darker fabrics on one side and lighter fabrics on the other, make 24 blocks.

Round 1

Light   Dark   Dark   Light

Round 2

Light   Dark   Dark   Light

Stitch blocks into 4 borders, rotated as shown. Press. Stitch one to each side of quilt, dark side toward center of quilt. Press. Applique hearts to centers of corner squares. Stitch one to each end of each remaining border, making sure dark side of each border will be on inside when stitched to quilt. Stitch borders to top and bottom of quilt. Press.

Make 4

6. LAYER & QUILT: Piece backing to same size as batting. Layer and quilt as desired. Trim backing and batting even with top.

7. BIND: Stitch binding strips end to end. Press in half lengthwise, wrong sides together. Bind quilt using ⅜" seam allowance.

Snowberries

Continued from page 16

3. BORDER 1: Stitch 5"-wide strips end to end. Press. Cut 2 to same length as quilt. Stitch to sides of quilt. Press. Repeat at top and bottom with 5¾"-wide strips.

4. BORDER 2: Make 156 half-square triangle units. Press. Stitch into pairs to make 78 double units. Press. Make 2 side borders with 22 double units each. Press. Repeat with 17 double units for top and bottom, adding red squares to each end. Stitch side borders to quilt. Press. Stitch top and bottom borders to quilt. Press.

5. BORDER 3: Stitch strips end to end. Press. Cut 2 to same length as quilt. Stitch to sides of quilt. Press. Repeat at top and bottom.

6. LAYER & QUILT: Piece backing vertically to same size as batting. Layer and quilt as desired. Trim backing and batting even with top.

7. BIND: Stitch binding strips end to end. Press in half lengthwise, wrong sides together. Bind quilt using ⅜" seam allowance.

 Make 156

Sides - Make 2 - 22 double units

Top/Bottom - Make 2 - 17 double units + squares at each end

Juniper & Pine

48 x 58"   10" Block   Photo on page 27

Yardage
Choose fabric with 40-42" usable width.

Black   3 yd

Greens   ⅜ yd each of 6 fabrics - large squares in blocks, block & border triangles, applique

Reds   ¼ yd each of 3 fabrics - blocks, border, applique

Backing   3¼ yd

Batting   54 x 64"

Trims   24 buttons - ¼" - berries
           beads - centers of poinsettias

Cutting
Cut strips selvage to selvage.
  *Cut in half diagonally.
  Applique patterns on page 45.

Black   48 pieces 1½ x 5" - block center bars

           48 squares 2" - block corners

           *96 squares 2⅜" - triangle units in blocks

           *37 squares 2⅞" - triangle units in Border 2

           4 strips 1½" wide - Border 1

           5 strips 6½" wide - Border 3

           6 strips 2½" wide - binding

Greens   48 squares 3½" - large squares in blocks

           *96 squares 2⅜" - triangle units in blocks

           *37 squares 2⅞" - triangle units in Border 2

Reds   12 squares 1½" - block centers

           4 squares 2½" - Border 2 corners

Applique   1 piece 3 x 14" for vine, 32 large leaves, 16 holly leaves, 4 poinsettias - trace directly from book

Directions
Use ¼" seam allowance unless otherwise noted.

1. BLOCKS: Make 12 blocks following diagrams. Press.

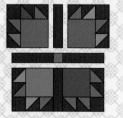

Make 192

Make 48

Make 48

Make 48

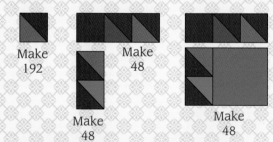

Make 12

2. ASSEMBLE: Stitch blocks into horizontal rows. Press. Stitch rows together. Press.

3. BORDER 1: Cut 2 strips to same length as quilt. Stitch to sides of quilt. Press. Repeat at top and bottom.

4. BORDER 2: Make 74 half-square triangle units. Press. Stitch into borders as shown. Note the change of direction at or near the center of each border. Stitch side borders to quilt. Press. Stitch red squares to each end of top and bottom borders. Press. Stitch top and bottom borders to quilt. Press. Another diagram on page 36.

Sides - Make 2 using 21 half-square triangle units

Top & Bottom - Make 2 using 16 half-square triangle units

Continued on page 36

Couch Topper

60x40″ 12″ Block Photo on page 29

Yardage Choose fabric with 40-42″ usable width.

Black	2⅜ yd	- overhang, blocks
Red	¼ yd	- frames
Green	⅓ yd	- sashing
Reds	¼ yd each of 3-4	- blocks, berries
Greens	¼ yd each of 3-4	- blocks, leaves
Binding	⅝ yd	
Backing	2¾ yd	
Batting	64x44″	

Cutting Cut strips selvage to selvage.
*Cut in half diagonally.
Applique patterns on page 44.

Black	overhang	1 piece 24½x60½″ cut in one piece parallel to selvage
	bottom	1 piece 2x60½″ cut in one piece parallel to selvage
	sides	2 pieces 2x15½″
	blocks	16 squares 2½″ - corners
		*16 squares 2⅞″ - corner units
		32 pieces 2½x4½″ - side units
Red	frames	8 pieces 1x12½″ - sides
		8 pieces 1x13½″ - top/bottom
Green	sashing	5 pieces 1½x13½″ - verticals
		3 strips 1½″ wide - horizontals
Reds	blocks	*16 squares 2⅞″ - corner units
	blocks	32 squares 2½″ - side units
Greens	blocks	4 squares 4½″ - centers
		16 squares 2½″ - corner units
Applique		18 berries, 6 sets leaves - trace directly from book
Binding		6 strips 2½″ wide

Directions
Use ¼″ seam allowance unless otherwise noted.

1. BLOCKS: Make 4 blocks following diagrams. Press.

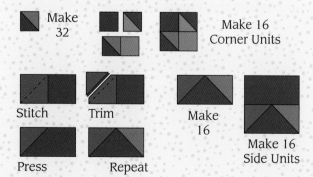

Make 32

Make 16 Corner Units

Stitch   Trim   Make 16

Press   Repeat   Make 16 Side Units

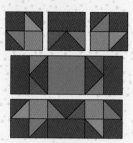

Make 4

2. FRAMES: Stitch short frame pieces to sides. Press. Stitch long frame pieces to top and bottom. Press.

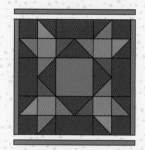

3. SASHING: Stitch blocks together with 13½″ sashing pieces between them and at each end. Press. Stitch long sashing strips end to end. Press. Cut 2 pieces 57½″ long. Stitch to top and bottom of row of blocks. Press.

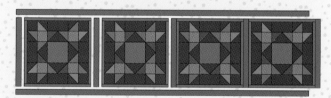

4. OVERHANG: Applique 6 sets of holly leaves and berries to one long edge of overhang, leaving approximately 1″ of background at bottom and 6″ at side edges. Stitch black side pieces to sides of row of blocks. Press. Stitch black bottom piece to row of blocks. Press. Stitch overhang to row of blocks. Press. Diagram on page 34.

Continued on page 34

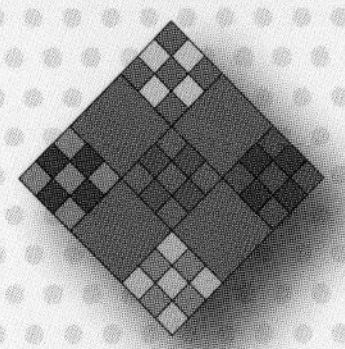

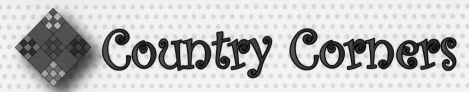

Country Corners

52x52″ 9″ Block Photo on page 31

Yardage
Choose fabric with 40-42″ usable width.

Corner 9-patch units	⅛ yd each of 2 reds, 4 greens, 1 brown, 1 blue ¼ yd each of 2 tans
Center 9-patch units	¼ yd each of 2 reds
Block setting squares	⅙ yd each of 3 reds, 2 greens
Large setting squares & triangles	1 yd red
Border 1	½ yd red
Border 2	⅛ yd each of 6 fabrics choose 6 of the 9-patch fabrics to repeat in this border & get an additional ⅛ yd of each
Border 3	¾ yd red
Binding	⅝ yd
Backing	3½ yd
Batting	58x58″

Cutting
Cut strips selvage to selvage.
*Cut in half diagonally.
**Cut in quarters diagonally.

Corner 9-patches	2 strips 1½″ wide of each red & green, brown, blue 4 strips 1½″ wide of each tan
Center 9-patches	3 strips 1½″ wide of each fabric
Block setting squares	total of 36 squares 3½″ in sets of 4 from the same fabric
Large setting squares & triangles	4 squares 9½″ *2 squares 7¼″ **2 squares 14″
Border 1	5 strips 2⅜″ wide
Border 2	2 strips 1½″ wide of each fabric
Border 3	5 strips 4½″ wide
Binding	6 strips 2½″ wide

Directions
Use ¼″ seam allowance unless otherwise noted.

1. BLOCKS
Corner 9-patch units: Cut all strips in half, to 20″ long. For each color combination named below, make one Strip Set 1 for top and bottom rows of 9-patch, and one Strip Set 2 for center row of 9 patch. Press. Cut 1½″ segments. Stitch segments into 9-patch units. Press. Make a total of 36.

Green & tan (tan in corners)
Green & tan (tan in corners)
Green & green (lighter green in corners)
Brown & tan (brown in corners)
Red & tan (tan in corners)
Blue & red (red in corners)

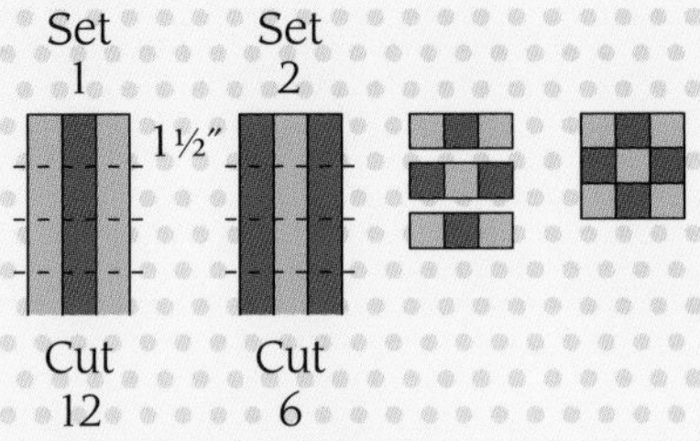

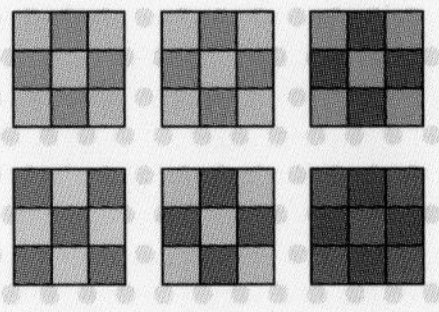
Corners
Make 6 of each

Center 9-patch units: Make strip sets with full-length strips. Press. Cut segments. Stitch segments into 9-patch units. Press.

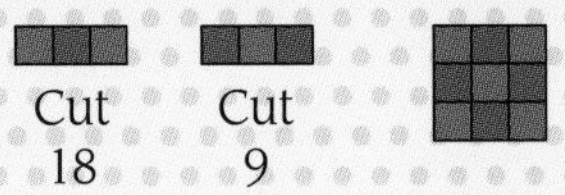

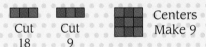

Centers
Make 9

Stitch 9-patch units and block setting squares into blocks, red/red 9-patches in centers. Press. Make 9. Note: Photo varies slightly from directions. Refer to diagrams on page 37 for placement of 9-patches, or place 9-patches in blocks as desired.

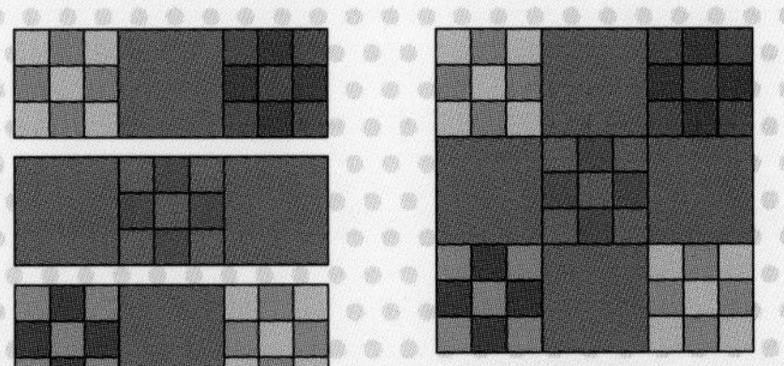
Make 9

2. ASSEMBLE: Stitch blocks, setting squares, and setting triangles into diagonal rows. Press. Stitch rows together. Press. Diagram on page 37.

Continued on page 37

Country Corners   p 30
Country Corners Pillow   p 36

Juniper & Pine Apron

8⅜″ Block   Photo on page 27

Yardage
Choose fabric with 40-42″ usable width.

Apron, lining	1¾ yd red
Trim, ties, pocket	¾ yd black
Trim, pocket	¼ yd green
	⅛ yd each of 2 greens

Cutting
Cut strips selvage to selvage.
*Cut in half diagonally.

Red	cut 2 using apron pattern, page 47	
	*10 squares 2⅛″ - bottom patchwork	
Black	1 strip 1½″ - top trim	
	1 strip 3″ - bottom trim	
	3 strips 2½″ - ties	
	*10 squares 2⅛″ - bottom patchwork	
Trim	1 strip 1½″ - from ¼-yd piece of green	
Pocket	red	1 square 1⅜″ - center
	black	4 pieces 1⅜ x 4¼″ - center bars
		*8 squares 2⅛″ - triangle units
		4 squares 1¾″ - corners
		1 square 8⅞″ - pocket lining
	green	4 squares 3″ - large squares - cut from ¼-yd piece of green
	greens	*8 squares 2⅛″ - triangle units - cut from ⅛-yd pieces of green

Directions
Use ¼″ seam allowance unless otherwise noted.
Press all seams as soon as they are stitched.

1. TRIM & BOTTOM PATCHWORK: Cut 1″ from top edge of apron front and 4¾″ from bottom edge of apron front. Cut top trim piece to same width as top edge of apron. Stitch to top of apron. For patchwork strip at bottom of apron, make 20 half-square triangle units, stitch into 10 double units as shown, then stitch 10 double units together. Stitch to bottom edge of apron. Stitch green trim to patchwork strip. Stitch 3″ black trim to green trim.

2. POCKET: Make block following diagrams. Press. Pin block and lining square right sides together and stitch around pocket, leaving an opening on one side for turning. Clip corners, turn right side out, and press. Stitch opening closed. Quilt minimally in the ditch to hold lining to pocket. Pin pocket to right side of apron front 3″ down from top edge, centered from left to right. Topstitch side and bottom edges.

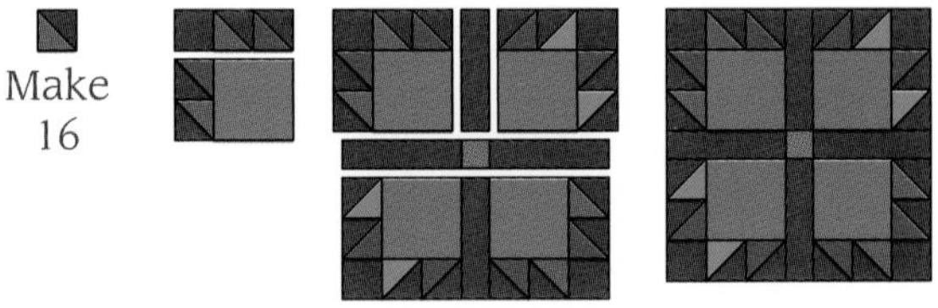

Make 16

3. TIES: To make side ties, fold 2 strips lengthwise, right sides together, and stitch long side and one short end. Clip corners. Turn right side out. Press. Pin unfinished ends of waist ties between marks on sides of apron, right sides together, raw edges even. To make neck ties, cut remaining strip in half lengthwise and repeat stitching and turning directions. Pin unfinished ends between marks on top edge of apron.

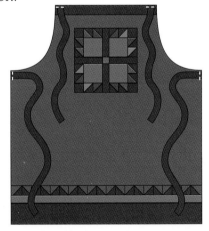

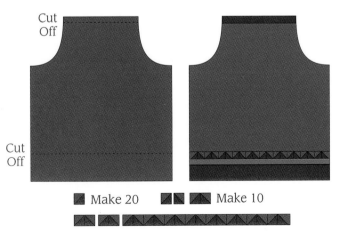

Cut Off

Cut Off

■ Make 20   ◪◩ Make 10

4. FINISH: Pin ties to apron front to keep them out of seams. Pin apron front and lining right sides together. Stitch around apron, catching raw ends of ties in seam and leaving an opening on one side for turning. Clip corners, turn right side out, and press. Stitch opening closed. Topstitch edges of apron if desired.

Poinsettia Table Runner

12x66″ 10″ Block Photo on page 27

Materials Choose fabric with 40-42″ usable width.

Black	1¾ yd
Greens	¼ yd - large squares
	⅙ yd each of 3 or more fabrics - triangle units
Reds	⅙-¼ yd pieces of 3 fabrics or scraps up to 9x9″
Backing	1 yd
Batting	16x70″
Trims	beads for flower centers

Cutting Cut strips selvage to selvage.
*Cut in half diagonally.
Applique pattern on page 45.

Black	3 strips 1½″ wide - sides
	2 rectangles 2½x12½″ - ends
	*1 square 9⅜″ - ends
	4 strips 1½″ wide - facing
	32 squares 3⅞″ - prairie points
	20 pieces 1½x 5″ - block center bars
	20 squares 2″ - block corners
	*40 squares 2⅜″ - block triangle units
Greens	20 squares 3½″ - large squares
	*40 squares 2⅜″ - triangle units
Reds	5 squares 1½″ - block centers
Applique	2 poinsettias - trace directly from book

Directions
Use ¼″ seam allowance unless otherwise noted.

1. BLOCKS: Make 5 blocks following diagrams. Press.

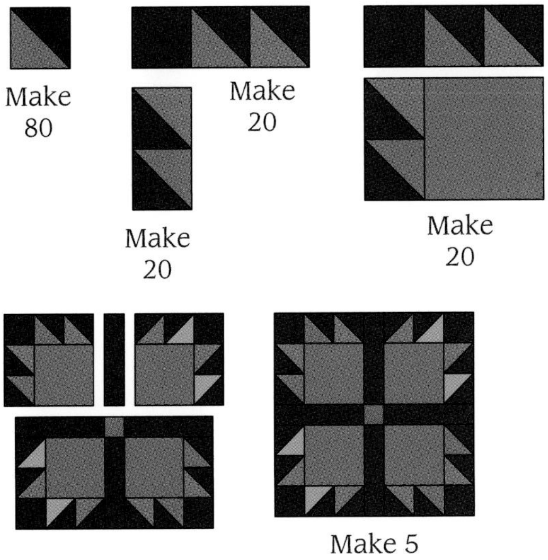

Make 80
Make 20
Make 20
Make 20
Make 5

2. ASSEMBLY: Stitch blocks into a row. Press. Stitch 1½″ strips end to end. Press. Cut 2 pieces 50½″ long. Stitch one to each long side of row of blocks. Press. Stitch rectangles to each end. Press. Stitch large triangles to each end. Press.

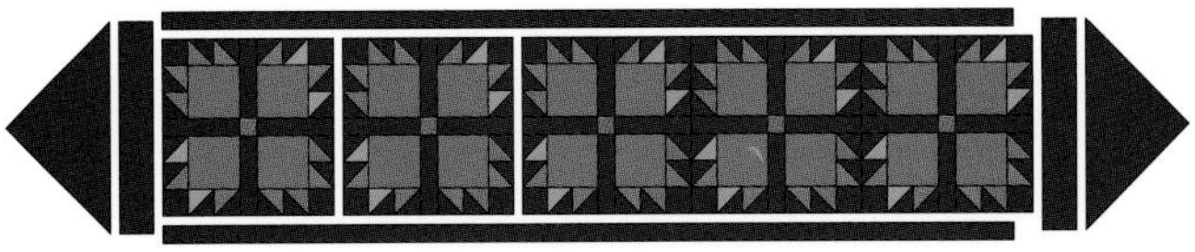

3. APPLIQUE: Applique poinsettias to each end of table runner, overlapping seam between large triangle and rectangle.

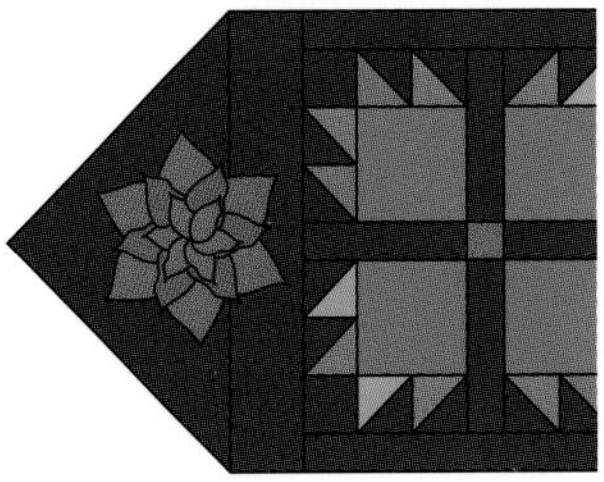

4. LAYER & QUILT: Piece backing to same size as batting. Layer and quilt as desired. Trim backing and batting even with top.
5. PRAIRIE POINTS: Fold and press 32 prairie points for edging.

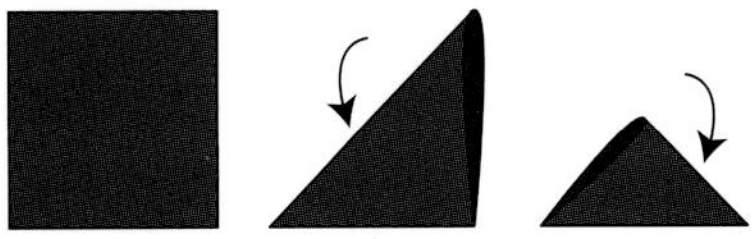

Pin prairie points to long sides of table runner, raw edges even, slipping one inside the next to space them evenly. They will overlap each other close to ¼″ seam line. The folded edge of the ones at each end should match seam intersections so corners will be smooth when turned. Baste prairie points in place 3/16″ from edge.

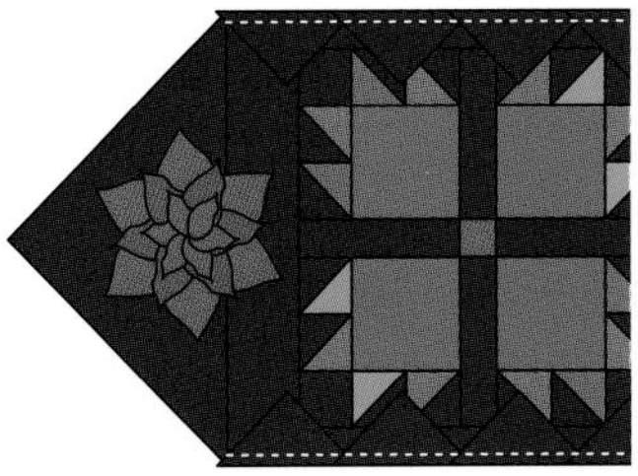

Continued on page 35

Noel Pillow

For 28x14″ pillow form   Photo on page 29

Materials Choose fabric with 40-42″ usable width.

Background	⅜ yd black
Border	⅙ yd green
Border	¼ yd red
Backing for quilting	⅝ yd
Applique	⅛-¼ yd pieces
	or scraps up to 7x7″
Envelope back	1 yd
Batting	32x18″
Pillow form	28x14″ - Fairfield
Trims	seven ½″ buttons - tree
Velcro® strip	⅙ yd

Cutting Applique patterns on page 44.

Black	1 piece 9½x25½″
Green	2 pieces 1½x25½″
Red	2 pieces 2x11½″
	2 pieces 2x28½″
Backing for quilting	1 piece 32x18″
Applique	NOEL, 1 tree, 1 set holly, 4 circles - make 200% copies of letters, then trace - trace all others directly from book
Envelope back	2 pieces 19x28½″

Directions
Use ¼″ seam allowance unless otherwise noted.

1. BORDERS: Stitch green pieces to top and bottom of black rectangle. Press. Stitch short red strips to sides. Press. Stitch long red pieces to top and bottom. Press.

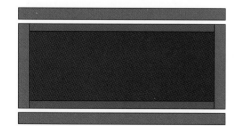

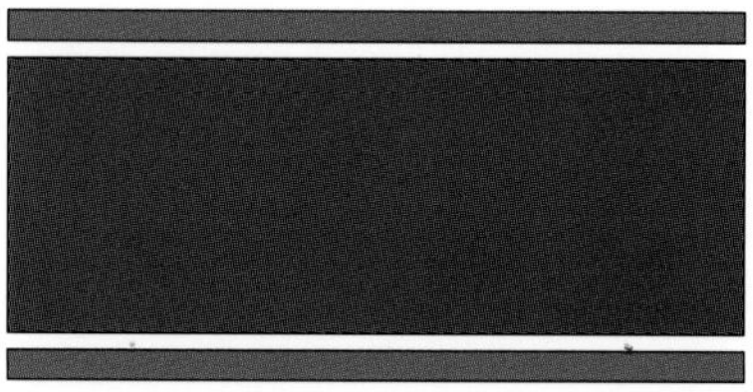

2. APPLIQUE: Applique letters, tree, holly, and circles to pillow front.

3. LAYER & QUILT: Layer backing, batting, and top. Quilt as desired. Trim backing and batting even with top. Stitch buttons to tree.

4. ENVELOPE BACK: Press pieces in half lengthwise, wrong sides together (9½x28½″). Place both on right side of pillow front, raw edges matching, folded edges overlapping in center. Stitch around entire outside edge. Clip corners, turn right side out. Stitch buttons to tree. Place pillow cover on pillow form and work out placement for Velcro®. Mark placement. Remove pillow form. Stitch Velcro® to pillow opening. Replace pillow cover on pillow form.

Couch Topper
Continued from page 28

5. LAYER & QUILT: Piece backing to same size as batting. Layer and quilt as desired. Trim backing and batting even with top.

6. BIND: Stitch binding strips end to end. Press in half lengthwise, wrong sides together. Bind topper using ⅜″ seam allowance.

Noel Tree Skirt

52″ diameter   Photos on pages 19, 29

Materials   Choose fabric with 40-42″ usable width.

Wedges   1½ yd each of 2 reds
Ties   ⅜ yd green
Applique   ⅛-¼ yd pieces or scraps up to 7x7″
Binding   ¾ yd
Backing   3⅜ yd
Batting   56x56″
Trims   7 buttons - ½″ - tree

Cutting   Cut strips selvage to selvage.
Wedge pattern on page 46.
Applique patterns on page 44.

Wedges   cut all from single layer:
    9 from 1st red fabric
    9 in reverse from 2nd red fabric
Ties   4 pieces 4½x21″
Applique   NOEL, 7 sets holly, 1 tree, 4 circles - make 200% copies of letters, then trace - trace all others directly from book
Binding   **bias** strips 2½″ **wide** pieced to 250″ long

Directions

Use ¼″ seam allowance unless otherwise noted.

1. WEDGES: Make 9 wedges with one of each red. Press. Stitch wedges together in three sets of three. Press. Stitch three sets together, leaving one seam open. Press.

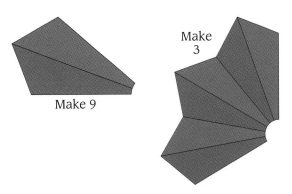

Make 3

Make 9

2. APPLIQUE: Stitch appliques in positions shown, keeping them an inch or more from raw edges.

Leave
Open

3. FINISH: See Steps 3-5 on page 4.

Poinsettia Table Runner

Continued from page 33

6. FACING & TRIM: Stitch facing strips end to end. Press seam allowances open. Press ½″ to wrong side on one long edge. Place unpressed edge of facing strip right sides together with raw edge of runner and stitch, pivoting at seam intersections of corners. Trim the 6 corners. Fold facing to back of runner so prairie points extend at edge. Hand stitch pressed edge to back of runner, mitering the corners. Stitch beads to centers of poinsettias.

Juniper & Pine

Continued from page 26

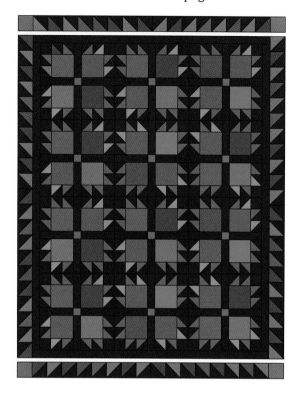

5. BORDER 3: Stitch border strips end to end. Press. Cut 2 pieces the same length as quilt. Stitch to sides of quilt. Press. Repeat at top and bottom. Fuse web to back of vine fabric. Cut 8 pieces ¼ x 12″. Place vine and leaves using photo and diagrams as guides. Fuse and applique.

6. LAYER & QUILT: Piece backing horizontally to same size as batting. Layer and quilt as desired. Trim backing and batting even with top.

7. BIND & ADD TRIMS: Stitch binding strips end to end. Press in half lengthwise, wrong sides together. Bind quilt using ⅜″ seam allowance. Stitch 3 buttons to base of each set of holly leaves. Stitch beads to centers of poinsettias.

Country Corners Pillow

16″   Photo on page 31

Materials Choose fabric with 40-42″ usable width.

Nine-patch units	⅛ yd each of 8-10 fabrics
Setting squares	⅙ yd red
Border 1	⅛ yd blue
Border 2	¼ yd red
Envelope back	⅝ yd
Backing for quilting	⅝ yd
Batting	18 x 18″
Pillow form	16″

Cutting Cut strips selvage to selvage.

Nine-patches	1½″ squares - 45 total
Setting squares	4 squares 3½″
Border 1	1 strip 1½″ wide
Border 2	2 strips 3″ wide
Envelope back	2 pieces 16½ x 20″

Directions

Use ¼″ seam allowance unless otherwise noted.

1. BLOCK: Make 5 nine-patches with 1½″ squares. Press. Stitch into rows with setting squares. Stitch rows together. Press.

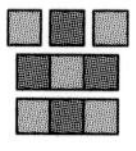

Make 5

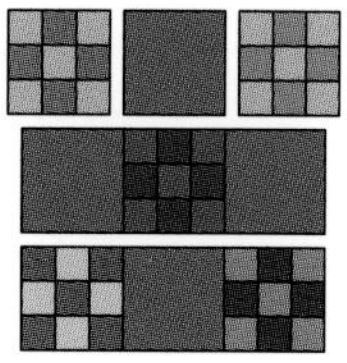

Continued on page 37

Country Corners

Continued from page 30

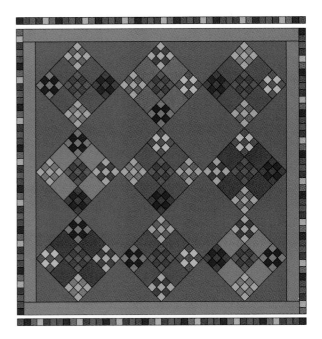

3. BORDER 1: Cut 2 pieces the same length as quilt. Stitch to sides of quilt. Press. Stitch remaining 3 strips end to end. Press. Cut 2 pieces to fit top and bottom of quilt. Stitch to quilt. Press.

4. BORDER 2: Make 2 strip sets as shown. Press. Crosscut into 1½″ segments (30 needed). Stitch segments together end to end to make 2 side borders of 42 squares each (7 segments) and 2 top/bottom borders of 44 squares each (8 segments with 4 squares removed from end of last one). Press. Stitch side borders to quilt. Press. Stitch top and bottom borders to quilt. Press.

5. BORDER 3: Stitch strips end to end. Press. Cut 2 the same length as quilt. Stitch to sides of quilt. Press. Repeat at top and bottom.

6. LAYER & QUILT: Piece backing to same size as batting. Layer and quilt as desired. Trim backing and batting even with top.

7. BIND: Stitch binding strips end to end. Press in half lengthwise, wrong sides together. Bind quilt using ⅜″ seam allowance.

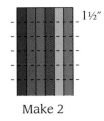

1½″

Make 2

Sides - Make 2 - 42 Squares

Top/Bottom - Make 2 - 44 Squares

Country Corners Pillow

Continued from page 36

2. BORDERS: Cut two Border 1 pieces to same length as block. Stitch to sides. Press. Repeat at top and bottom. Repeat with Border 2 strips.

3. QUILT: Cut quilting backing to same size as batting. Layer and quilt as desired. Trim backing and batting even with top.

4. ENVELOPE BACK: Fold pieces in half, wrong sides together, to 10x16½″. Place on right side of pillow front, raw edges matching, folded edges overlapping at center of pillow. Stitch around entire outside edge. Clip corners, turn right side out, and press.

5. Insert pillow form.

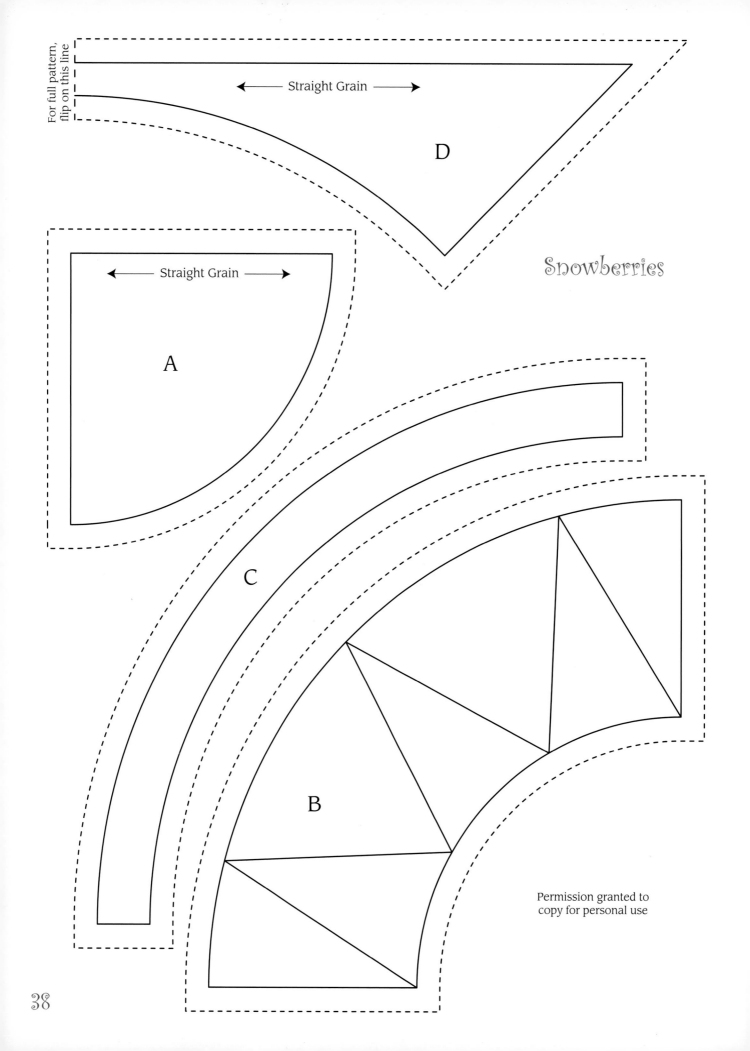

For full pattern, flip on this line

Straight Grain

D

Snowberries

Straight Grain

A

C

B

Permission granted to copy for personal use

38

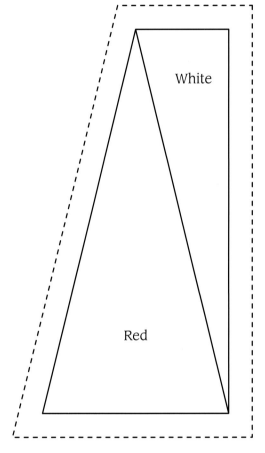

White

Red

Left End Section

Right End Section
on page 47

Right End Section
on page 47

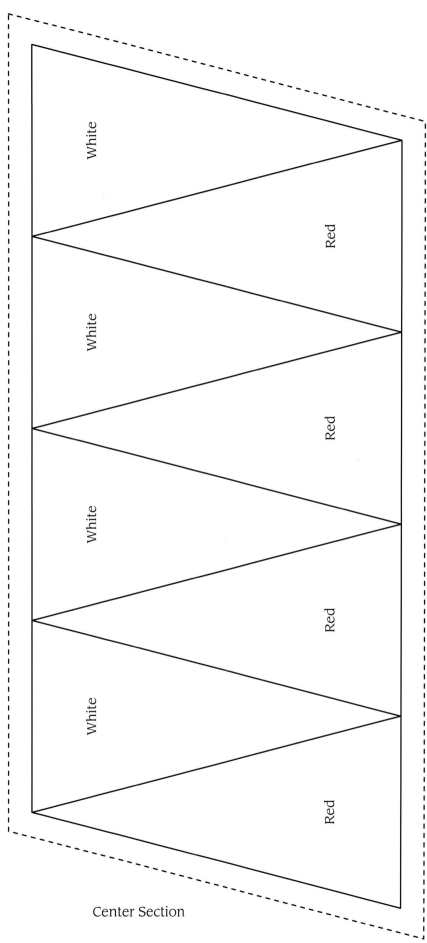

White

Red

White

Red

White

Red

White

Red

Center Section

Santa
Door Topper
Trace all pieces at 100%

Santa
Card Hanger
Trace all pieces at 100%

Ho! Ho! Ho!
Copy all pieces (except hearts
& stars) at 200% & trace

Santa Stocking
Copy Santa at 200% & trace
Trace stars at 100%

Quilt or applique
on dotted lines

Gingerbread
Wall Quilt
100%

Santa Door Topper
100%

Santa
Stocking
100%

Santa Card Hanger
100%

Ho! Ho! Ho!
100%

Santa Door
Topper
100%

Santa
Card
Hanger
100%

Tree
Stocking
100%

Ho! Ho! Ho!
Corner Squares
100%

Ho! Ho! Ho!
Tree 100%

Use permanent marker,
embroidery floss,
or beads for eyes–
applique cheeks or
use blush makeup

For buckle detail, use machine
satin stitch, embroidery
floss, or omit

Patterns are for fusible web
applique, reversed for tracing
and no seam allowances added

Permission granted to
copy for personal use

40

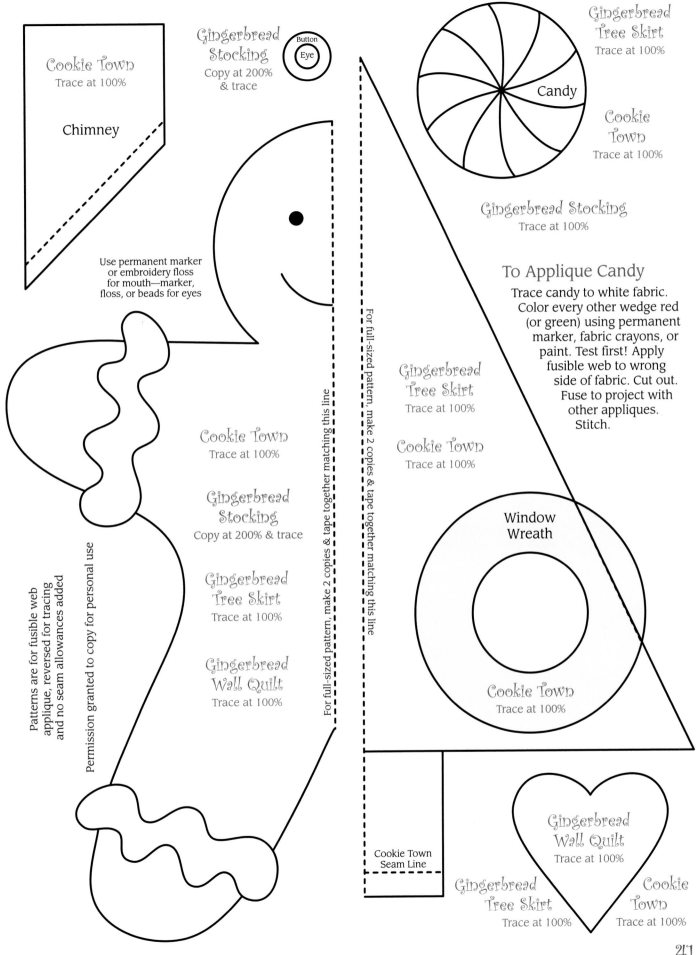

Cookie Town
Trace at 100%

Chimney

Gingerbread
Stocking
Copy at 200%
& trace

Button
Eye

Gingerbread
Tree Skirt
Trace at 100%

Candy

Cookie
Town
Trace at 100%

Gingerbread Stocking
Trace at 100%

Use permanent marker
or embroidery floss
for mouth—marker,
floss, or beads for eyes

To Applique Candy

Trace candy to white fabric.
Color every other wedge red
(or green) using permanent
marker, fabric crayons, or
paint. Test first! Apply
fusible web to wrong
side of fabric. Cut out.
Fuse to project with
other appliques.
Stitch.

Cookie Town
Trace at 100%

Gingerbread
Stocking
Copy at 200% & trace

Gingerbread
Tree Skirt
Trace at 100%

Gingerbread
Wall Quilt
Trace at 100%

Gingerbread
Tree Skirt
Trace at 100%

Cookie Town
Trace at 100%

Window
Wreath

Cookie Town
Trace at 100%

Patterns are for fusible web
applique, reversed for tracing
and no seam allowances added

Permission granted to copy for personal use

For full-sized pattern, make 2 copies & tape together matching this line

For full-sized pattern, make 2 copies & tape together matching this line

Cookie Town
Seam Line

Gingerbread
Wall Quilt
Trace at 100%

Gingerbread
Tree Skirt
Trace at 100%

Cookie
Town
Trace at 100%

41

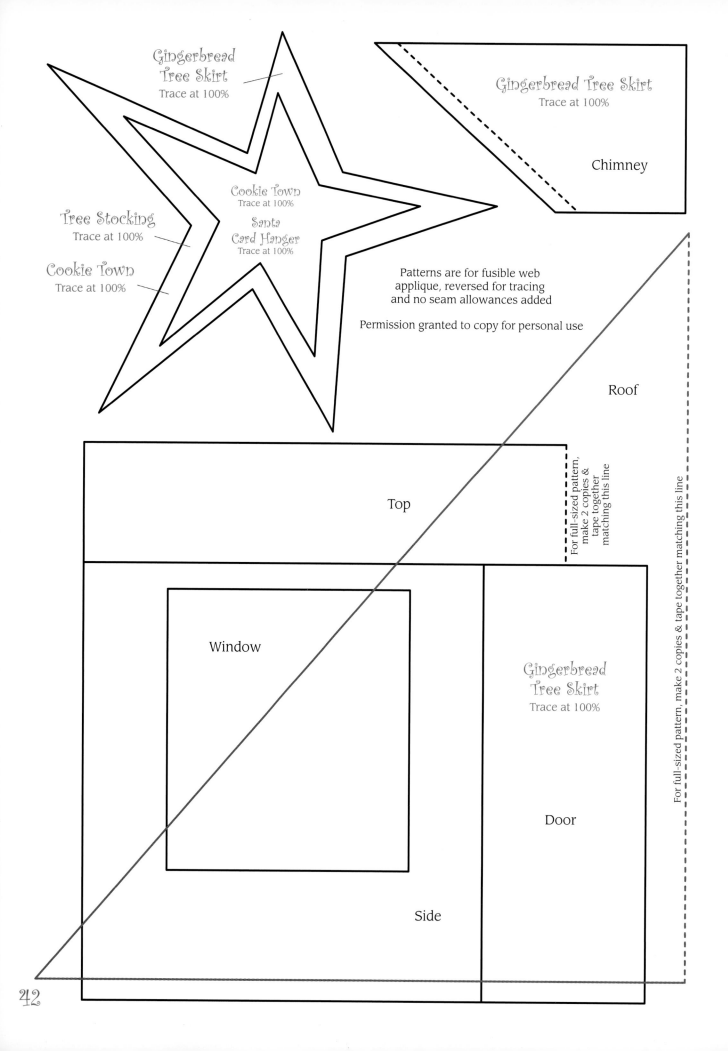

Gingerbread
Tree Skirt
Trace at 100%

Gingerbread Tree Skirt
Trace at 100%

Chimney

Cookie Town
Trace at 100%

Santa
Card Hanger
Trace at 100%

Tree Stocking
Trace at 100%

Cookie Town
Trace at 100%

Patterns are for fusible web
applique, reversed for tracing
and no seam allowances added

Permission granted to copy for personal use

Roof

Top

For full-sized pattern,
make 2 copies &
tape together
matching this line

Window

Gingerbread
Tree Skirt
Trace at 100%

Door

Side

For full-sized pattern, make 2 copies & tape together matching this line

ABCDEFG
HIJKLMN
OPQRSTU
VWXYZ

Stockings
For short names, copy
at 200% & trace
Copy at smaller percentages
for longer names

To Make Full-sized Snowflake Pattern

Fold a 7" square of paper in half, in half again,
then in thirds. Reduce bulk by making the last
two folds accordion-style. Make a mark on the
outside segment. Unfold paper. Place marked
segment over pattern below, lining up dotted
lines on folds and dot on center of paper
square. Trace solid lines only. Refold with
tracing on outside and cut out on line.

Santa
Card Hanger
Trace at 100%

Cookie Town
Trace at 100%

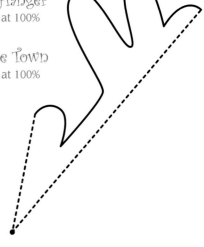

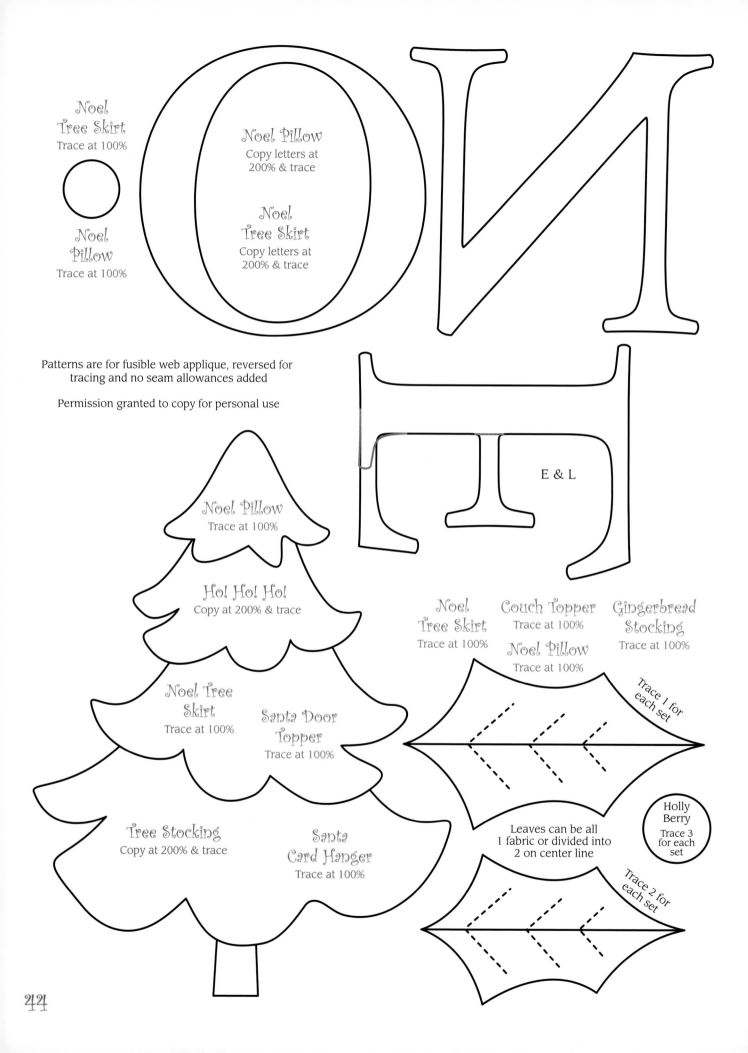

Noel
Tree Skirt
Trace at 100%

Noel Pillow
Copy letters at
200% & trace

Noel
Tree Skirt
Copy letters at
200% & trace

Noel
Pillow
Trace at 100%

Patterns are for fusible web applique, reversed for
tracing and no seam allowances added

Permission granted to copy for personal use

E & L

Noel Pillow
Trace at 100%

Ho! Ho! Ho!
Copy at 200% & trace

Noel Tree
Skirt
Trace at 100%

Santa Door
Topper
Trace at 100%

Tree Stocking
Copy at 200% & trace

Santa
Card Hanger
Trace at 100%

Noel
Tree Skirt
Trace at 100%

Couch Topper
Trace at 100%

Gingerbread
Stocking
Trace at 100%

Noel Pillow
Trace at 100%

Trace 1 for
each set

Trace 2 for
each set

Leaves can be all
1 fabric or divided into
2 on center line

Holly
Berry
Trace 3
for each
set

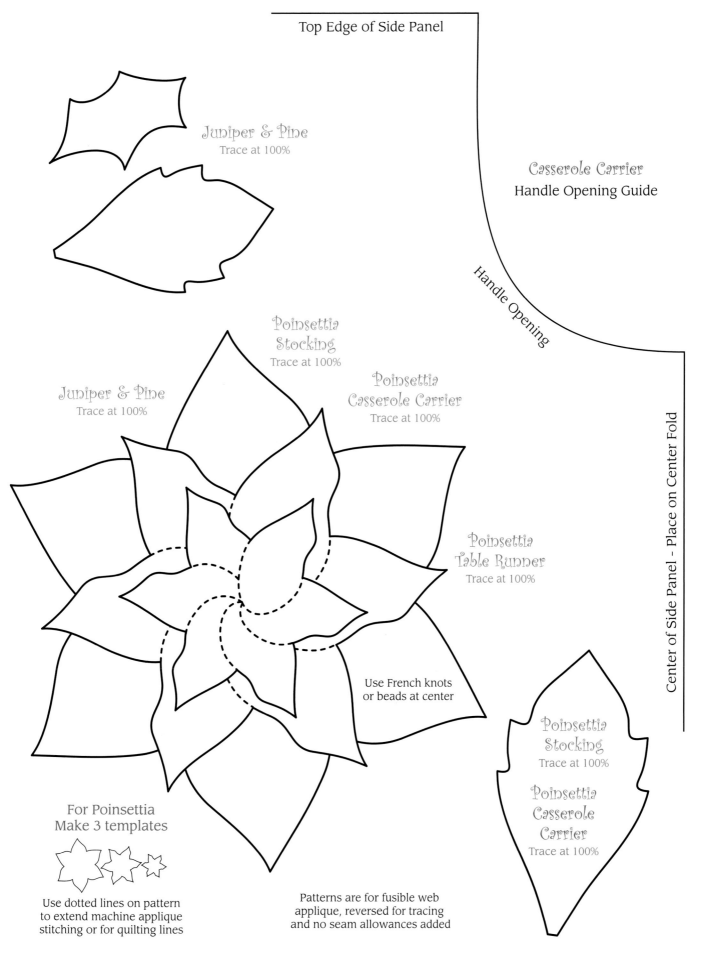

Top Edge of Side Panel

Juniper & Pine
Trace at 100%

Casserole Carrier
Handle Opening Guide

Handle Opening

Poinsettia
Stocking
Trace at 100%

Poinsettia
Casserole Carrier
Trace at 100%

Juniper & Pine
Trace at 100%

Poinsettia
Table Runner
Trace at 100%

Center of Side Panel – Place on Center Fold

Use French knots
or beads at center

Poinsettia
Stocking
Trace at 100%

Poinsettia
Casserole
Carrier
Trace at 100%

For Poinsettia
Make 3 templates

Use dotted lines on pattern
to extend machine applique
stitching or for quilting lines

Patterns are for fusible web
applique, reversed for tracing
and no seam allowances added

Permission granted to copy for personal use

45

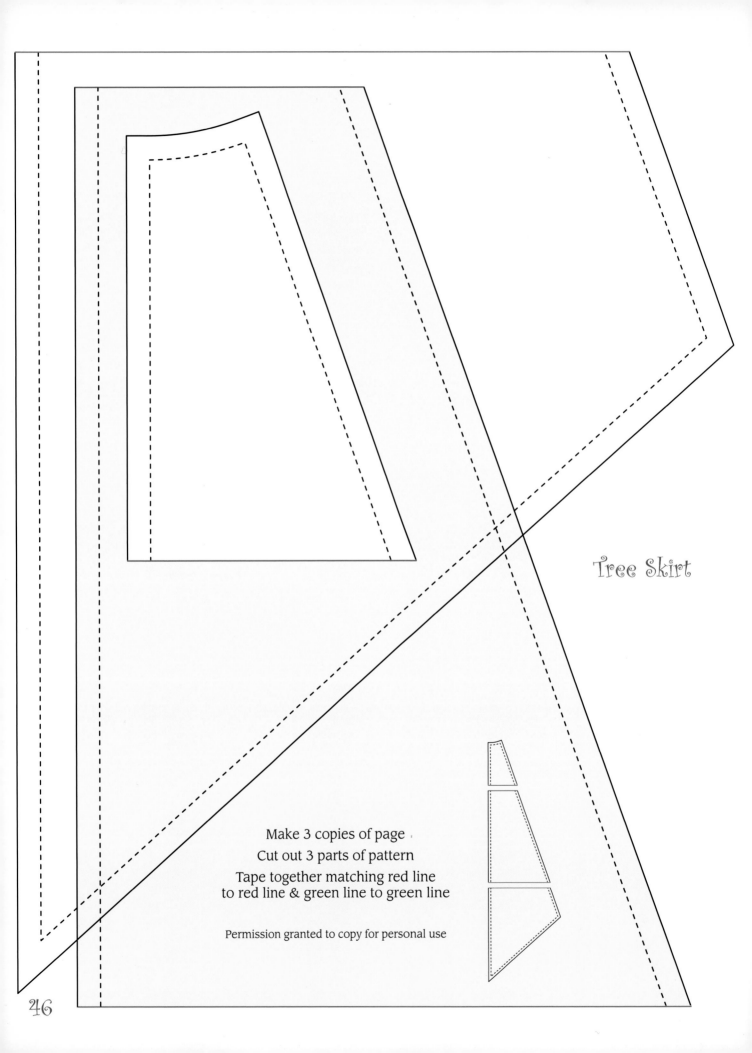

Tree Skirt

Make 3 copies of page
Cut out 3 parts of pattern
Tape together matching red line
to red line & green line to green line

Permission granted to copy for personal use

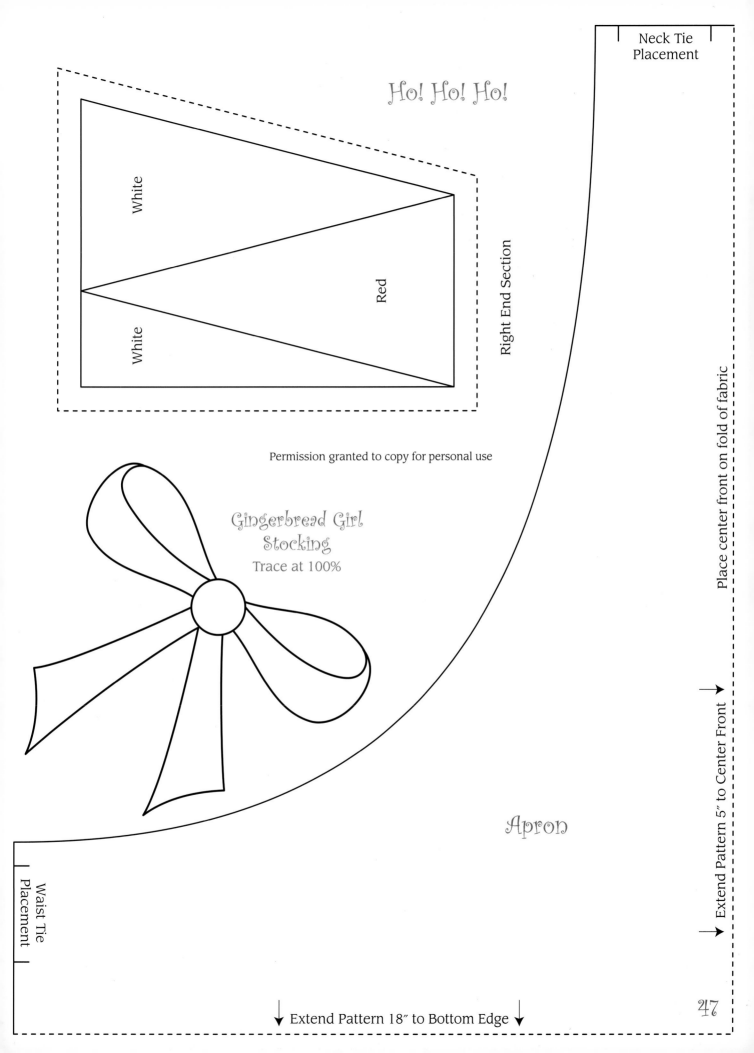

Ho! Ho! Ho!

White

Red

White

Right End Section

Permission granted to copy for personal use

Gingerbread Girl
Stocking
Trace at 100%

Place center front on fold of fabric

Extend Pattern 5″ to Center Front

Apron

Waist Tie
Placement

↓ Extend Pattern 18″ to Bottom Edge ↓

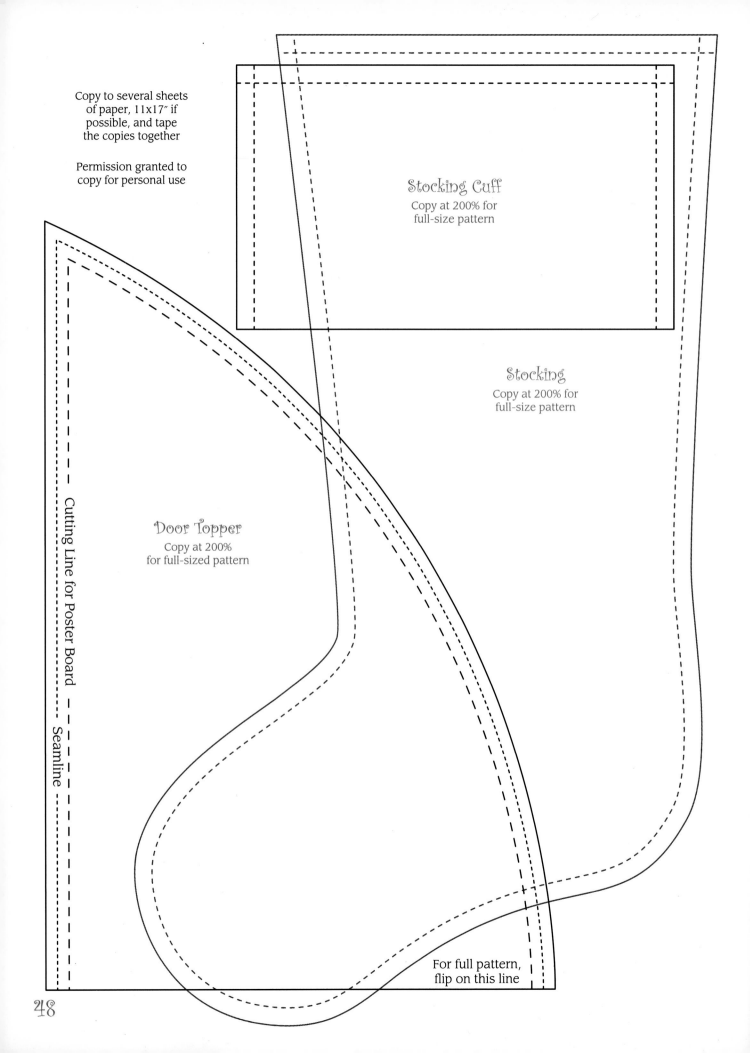

Copy to several sheets
of paper, 11x17″ if
possible, and tape
the copies together

Permission granted to
copy for personal use

Stocking Cuff
Copy at 200% for
full-size pattern

Stocking
Copy at 200% for
full-size pattern

Door Topper
Copy at 200%
for full-sized pattern

Cutting Line for Poster Board – – – – Seamline ......

For full pattern,
flip on this line